Not Even Wrong

CHANDLER & SHARP PUBLICATIONS IN ANTHROPOLOGY AND RELATED FIELDS

General Editors: L. L. Langness and Robert B. Edgerton

Not Even Wrong

Margaret Mead, Derek Freeman, and the Samoans

MARTIN ORANS

Chandler and Sharp Publishers, Inc.
Novato, California

The author and publisher are grateful to the following for authorization to reprint excerpts from their books:

Excerpts from *Coming of Age in Samoa* reprinted by permission of William Morrow and Company, Inc. Copyright ©1928, 1949, 1955, 1961, 1973 by Margaret Mead.

Excerpts reprinted by permission of the publisher from *Margaret Mead and Samoa: The Making and Unmaking of an Anthroplological Myth* by Derek Freeman, Cambridge, Mass.: Harvard University Press, copyright ©1983 by Derek Freeman.

Library of Congress Cataloging-in-Publication Data

Orans, Martin.
     Not Even Wrong: Margaret Mead, Derek Freeman, and the Samoans / Martin Orans.
          p.   cm. — (Chandler & Sharp publications in anthropology and related fields)
     Includes bibliographical references and index.
     ISBN 0-88316-564-3.
     1. Ethnology—Samoan Islands. 2. Ethnology—Methodology.
3. Mead, Margaret, 1901–1978. 4. Nature and nurture. 5. Freeman, Derek. 6. Samoan Islands—Social life and customs. I. Title.
II. Series.
GN671.S2073 1996
305.8'009961'3—dc20   95-39377

Edited by Barbara Metzger and Jonathan Sharp.
Book designed by Lisa Nishikawa and Jonathan Sharp.
Cover art by Daniel Pouesi.
Cover design by Jackie Gallagher Lange.
Composition by Page One Graphics / Lisa & David Nishikawa.

Contents

List of Tables

Acknowledgments

A few noble souls struggled through a first draft of this book and offered very helpful criticisms and suggestions for revision. I have done my best to respond to these criticisms and incorporate appropriate suggestions into the final version. Among such contributors I thank especially David Kronenfeld, Daniel Pouesi, Paul Shankman, David Strauss, and Max Yeh. Derek Freeman examined my first draft and pointed out a number of errors, since corrected; in spite of our profoundly different points of view I have benefited from his help.

I owe special thanks to Ali'itasi Summers, who provided translations of all handwritten documents in Samoan and whom I consulted repeatedly on subtle points of meaning.

To Mary Wolfskill of the Library of Congress, whose thoughtful and professionally skillful organization of the field materials of Margaret Mead made my research possible, I am profoundly grateful. In every respect she is an exemplar of public service at its best.

I thank my eldest daughter, Shima Orans, for reading my first draft and indicating by her response that it provided insufficient justification for anyone to care about the Mead-Freeman controversy. I have made an effort to remedy that deficiency.

I also thank a number of unnamed colleagues, friends, and

students who have listened to me while I wandered through the minefields of the Mead-Freeman dispute. Their comments have helped me to find my way. Included among these friends are my wife, who permitted this long-unfinished book to serve as an excuse for my leaving a number of things undone; I have recognized and appreciated her forbearance.

I thank my editor, Jonathan Sharp, whose careful proofreading, valuable suggestions, and patience have done much to improve this work. After so much improvement this work passed before the sharp eyes of Barbara Metzger whose blue pencil totally defaced the manuscript. Without her impeccable good taste and meticulous care I dread to think what would have happened. Finally, the author is most grateful to Rosemary Boyd who prepared the index.

Whatever foolishness remains in this book is of course my own, testifying to the limits of education.

Dana Point, California
April 1995

Not Even Wrong

Introduction

Occasionally a message carried by the media finds an audience so eager to receive it that it is willing to suspend all critical judgment and adopt the message as its own. So it was with Margaret Mead's celebrated *Coming of Age in Samoa.* First published in 1928 by William Morrow & Company, it eventually had numerous printings in several editions.[1] Other English language publishers have come out with their own editions; the international impact of the book may be indicated by the fact that it has been published in fifteen languages in addition to English. Generations of college students, including my own and several that I have taught, have read *Coming of Age* (hereafter *CA*) as an assigned reading in one course or another.

And what was it that the susceptible audience was so eager to find supported by the scientific establishment? The message that we awaited was confirmation of a vague ideological claim of the potency of culture as compared to biology in accounting for differences both within and between societies. Mead offered her study of a small island in the Samoan archipelago as a test case for the power of culture versus biology. She maintained that contrary to the views of such influential psychologists as G. Stanley Hall (1904), adolescence was not a biologically determined "period in which idealism flowered

1

and rebellion against authority waxed strong, a period during which difficulties and conflicts were absolutely inevitable" (1973:2). It was Mead's claim that none of these characteristics of adolescence were to be found in Samoa.[2] Since they were not universal, she argued, their prevalence in the United States ca. 1920 could not be biologically determined and therefore must be cultural. If the experience of adolescence was more dependent on culture than biology, then a host of other popularly accepted claims of biological determination might also be mistaken. As Mead put it, "One by one, aspects of behavior which we had been accustomed to consider invariable complements of our humanity were found to be merely a result of civilization, present in the inhabitants of one country, absent in another country, and this without a change of race" (1973:4). This perspective was meant as an antidote to racism and an answer to "the apostles of despair" who tell us that we cannot take steps to save our planet because "you can't change human nature" (1973:Preface:3).

Mead's message came well-packaged. Unlike most anthropological monographs, which are filled with custom and lack the experiential life of recognizable human beings, Mead's book provided numerous examples of adolescent girls living their lives within a cultural matrix, very much individuals with their own personalities and temperaments—this in spite of the fact that they were composites constructed, she informed us, to preserve anonymity. The work's popularity was of course also enhanced by its concern with sexuality on a South Seas isle, and those of us who were both receptive and young were not averse to hearing of a place where premarital sex was acceptable, accessible, and practiced with great fulfillment and without compunction. One grateful former student of mine returned years later to tell me that *CA* had proved positively therapeutic by freeing him from a pall of guilt regarding his own sexuality. Who would not be tempted to assign a work so liberating? Mead's message came at a time when many were not satisfied to raise their children traditionally as their parents had done—they knew how that turned out—but

wished instead to raise them according to the most enlight-
ened thought of the time. The imprimatur of science or what
passed for science constituted the highest authority on such
matters. Because Mead's work was deemed to possess authority, it became a guide for proper child rearing and justification
for sharing more sexual knowledge with children and a more
permissive attitude toward childhood and adolescent sexual
practice. Certainly all those who already held such views
welcomed Mead's validation.

As Derek Freeman has reminded us (1983a:98), eminent
scholars such as Havelock Ellis unreservedly praised Mead's
work (1929:25) and Bertrand Russell made use of her findings
in his popular work *Marriage and Morals* ("we are told [that
Samoans] when they have to go upon a journey, fully expect
their wives to console themselves for their absence"
[1957:132]). Most of Mead's anthropological colleagues
offered enthusiastic support. Her mentor, Franz Boas, "the
father of American anthropology" wrote in the book's
foreword, "She gives us a lucid and clear picture of the joys
and difficulties encountered by the young individual in a
culture so entirely different from our own. The results of her
painstaking investigation confirm the suspicion . . . that much
of what we ascribe to human nature is no more than a reaction
to the restraints put upon us by our civilisation" (Boas 1973:3).
Her other mentor and great friend, the eminent anthropologist Ruth Benedict, praised *CA* for its exemplification of the
power of culture to mold human behavior (Benedict 1928).
Nor was the support for her work confined to those with close
connections to Mead. The equally eminent Robert Lowie
reviewed *CA* in the foremost American anthropological
journal, *American Anthropologist,* and in spite of sensible
reservations regarding some of her unqualified generalizations
found her "graphic picture of Polynesian free love . . .
convincing" (1929:532). In conclusion he praised her methodology, pointing out that although her subject was "incom-
parably subtler than those which usually engage the
ethnographer's attention" she had "not merely added much

in the way of illuminating information but also illustrated a
new method of study that is bound to find followers and to
yield an even richer harvest" (534).

To be sure, there were a few dissonant voices in the
anthropological community. Lowell Holmes went to the very
villages where Mead had done her fieldwork and in his
dissertation and subsequent works took issue with some of
her specific findings and with her overemphasis on the
noncompetitive aspects of Samoan social life (Holmes 1957,
1958, 1987). However, he firmly supported Mead concerning
less adolescent "difficulties and conflicts" and a less restrictive
sexual regime. Some questions about Mead's claims regarding
the lack of premarital chastity among Samoan girls were raised
by Eleanor Gerber in her 1975 dissertation. She found in
her 1972–73 fieldwork that the prevailing practice was
"premarital chastity or the semblance of it" (1975:126). And
though her informants told her that formerly restrictions had
been tighter and punishment for violations more severe, she
concluded that the restrictions must in fact have become
greater in recent times, thus accepting Mead's findings.

Into this milieu of general acceptance of Mead's findings
Derek Freeman introduced his book-length critique of Mead's
Samoan research *Margaret Mead and Samoa: The Making and
Unmaking of an Anthropological Myth* (1983a). In the preface he
says that his work presents "detailed empirical evidence to
demonstrate that Mead's account of Samoan culture and
character is fundamentally in error" (1983a:xii). Among these
errors the most egregious would seem to be her diminution
of the "darker side of Samoan life" (278)—aggression,
violence, and rivalry—and her exaggeration of the degree of
sexual freedom of adolescent girls. These errors are fundamental because peace and sexual freedom are among the
characteristics of Samoan society that according to Mead
contribute to less conflicts for Samoan female adolescents.
Freeman does not explicitly claim that adolescent conflicts in
Samoa and the U.S. at the time were equal, but the message
is certainly that Mead has greatly underemphasized Samoan

difficulties. Implicitly he seems also to be arguing that these difficulties, like those alleged to plague American adolescents, are rooted in biology. Though he provides no explicit rationale for this claim, it seems to rest on his belief that Samoa, in spite of being culturally so different from the Western world, also has adolescents whose lives are filled with difficulties and conflicts.

Just as Mead set out to strike a blow for culture, Freeman through his "refutation" wished to make a case for what he called a new "paradigm," one in which culture and biology are interactive—"a synthesis" with "recognition of the radical importance of both the genetic and exogenetic and their interaction, both in the past history of the human species and in our problematic future" (1983a:302). Mead's case for the power of culture, given her assumptions, required a halcyon Samoa, free love, and little stress during adolescence; Freeman's case for biology, given his assumptions, required a more agonistic Samoa, greater sexual restrictions, and more adolescent stress. Each, then, wished to make of the Samoan evidence a charter for an outlook: Mead for the power of culture and Freeman for his interactive paradigm. Neither pretends that only the facts are at stake.

By the time Freeman's book appeared, Mead had been dead for five years, but she had long since become an institution. A complete bibliography of Mead's works published in 1976, two years before her death, listed 1,389 publications; though a few of these are interviews and not genuine publications, the number is staggering even for a career of some fifty years. These include ten books, countless articles in the professional journals of anthropology and other social sciences, and contributions to such varied nonprofessional journals as *The Nation*, the *New York Times Magazine*, the *Saturday Review*, *Look*, and *Redbook* (to which she contributed monthly articles from 1962 through 1975). The range of subjects covered in her books is as broad as anthropology but nowhere near as wide as the range of subjects treated in popular magazines, which include astrology and witches, family problems and bomb shelters (see Gordon 1976). In addition to her influence through publications, she was a tireless member of the international lecture circuit. She did voice recordings on records, tapes, and cassettes, served as narrator and/or consultant on a number of films, and is recorded on videotapes. She was made a member of the prestigious National Academy of Sciences and for many years served as a consultant to the federal government. Wilton Dillon notes that "perhaps no citizen in modern times has testified on so many different topics before different congressional committees" (1980:327).

Having become an international anthropological oracle, one might have thought that Mead would have been honored within the community of professional anthropologists. On the contrary, her colleagues were, I think, for the most part ambivalent about her accomplishments. This ambivalence was succinctly expressed in a recent conversation I had with an eminent American anthropologist; knowing that I had worked in Samoa, he asked me if Freeman's critique of Mead was correct, and I responded that in my opinion it was in some respects, though there were a number of subtle issues involved. When I had given him a brief account of some pertinent points, he reminded me in no uncertain terms that were it not for Mead, it is doubtful that my department of anthropology would even exist. At the same time, he said that he had never had much confidence in Mead's ethnographic findings and regarded her as primarily a popularizer. Whether merited or not, this was certainly a judgment widely held. However, her detractors on this score also recognized the contribution that her fame had made to the profession. Clearly Freeman's critique, apart from its defects, was bound to arouse the same anxiety as my offhand remarks—that the discrediting of Mead would do harm to the field of anthropology. In addition, many anthropologists, whatever their views on the quality of Mead's work, believed that her lifelong efforts to secure the understanding of the power of culture were surely on the side of the angels. Freeman's critique, with its avowed intention of giving the biological a greater role, was seen as reactionary and racist. Mead's work was a charter for an ideology that most anthropologists approved; Freeman's critique was seen as charter for an ideology that most anthropologists abhorred.

One might have thought that Freeman's critique, coming more than fifty years after Mead's investigation, would have been attended to only by a narrow range of historians of anthropology or specialists on Samoa. However, the media judged Mead's work and her reputation sufficient to make Freeman's book front-page news even before its publication (*New York Times,* Jan. 31, 1983). The article stressed the "nature versus nurture" aspect of the Mead-Freeman dispute and the connection between scholarship and ideology. In it, eminent physical anthropologist S. L. Washburn was quoted as saying that *CA* had "influenced the way people were brought up in this country." Quite appropriately he wondered, if Mead was as mistaken as Freeman says, "how many other people were collecting incorrect information and putting it out as fact." At the same time, he expressed some skepticism in noting that Freeman was "using this anti-Mead data to attack Boas."

In the same article, two biologists, chosen not for their knowledge of Samoa or even of cultural anthropology but presumably for their eminence and interest in the nature versus nurture controversy, also expressed their views on Freeman's not-yet-published book. The 1973 Nobel Prize winner for medicine, Nikolaas Tinbergen, famous for his work in ethology and behavioral biology, described it as "a masterpiece of modern scientific anthropology." Ernst Mayr, an eminent biologist and professor emeritus of zoology at Harvard, also gave it his blessing, saying that it "is not only a contribution to cultural anthropology, but it will also have a major impact on psychology and other aspects of human biology." How could Mead's work of 1928 have remained salient enough in the 1980s for Tinbergen and Mayr to regard its "refutation" as relevant to current scientific discourse? Surely the scientific community had progressed far beyond the heredity-environment dichotomy of the 1920s and had come to recognize the complex interaction between biological and experiential and environmental factors. The answer may be twofold: first, Mead's Samoan findings suggesting the plasticity of human behavior rather than the constraints exercised by biology had never been seriously challenged; in addition, perhaps these two biologists were not unhappy to see Mead's reputation tarnished a bit, since that reputation was intimately associated with support for an emphasis on culture that they no doubt regarded as overblown. Tinbergen and Mayr jumped on the Freeman bandwagon no doubt partly because they found the evidence compelling but also because they liked where it was going.

Books that resonate with some public interest leave an afterimage that is often not precisely or even substantially an accurate recollection of what they contain. The alterations made in memory may be a kind of simplification and unification like the completion of images that the Gestalt psychologists are so fond of demonstrating. A very striking example of this phenomenon is provided by a popular novel of the 1950s called *The Ugly American* (Lederer and Burdick, 1958). This didactic novel presented a message so resonant that the term "ugly American" entered the public vocabulary, coming to refer to Americans abroad who demonstrated by their insensitivity to all things foreign a vulgarity that did not reflect well upon our country. One thinks of Americans who judged other societies primarily by the quality of their toilet facilities; of Americans who expected everyone to speak English but made no effort to learn the language of others; of Americans who judged all customs by the degree to which they conformed with their own. All of these characteristics of the "ugly American" are indeed indicated in the novel; the inaccuracy introduced by memory is that the "ugly American" and an "ugly" native of the mythical country of Sarkhan are actually exemplars of the best that our country and Sarkhan can offer. The rough hands of the American hero, Homer Atkins, "always reminded him that he was an ugly man"

(1958:205). "Ugly" seems intended by the authors to be connected with manual work, straightforward honesty, bluntness, and other qualities characteristic of "the salt of the earth" and to contrast with the glitzy exterior of a number of insensitive Americans found in the novel—and, significantly, not the tourists whom the term "ugly American" came to designate but American diplomatic and aid representatives abroad. The novel was meant to be a warning about these representatives, whom the authors saw as contributing to our defeats in the cold war.

A similar distortion has taken place in our memory of *CA*. We remember a tranquil adolescence in a halcyon society; we remember South Sea island adolescents engaging in sex without adult restraints. We get the message and are delighted to know that somewhere such conditions really prevail. However, a careful rereading of *CA* indicates a much less halcyon society than we remembered; similarly, almost all of the adolescents who receive extended treatment in Mead's engaging account are far from untroubled, and the book indicates far more adult restraint on their sexuality than our afterimage.[3] Some of this distortion arises from the deft labeling, interpretation, and misleading generalizations Mead uses to buttress her case, some from our own preconceptions regarding South Sea isles and from our strong desire to believe in the existence of such a happy place and the ideology supported by its existence.

Since the publication of Freeman's book there have been an unprecedented number of reviews of the Mead-Freeman dispute in this country and abroad, including numerous rejoinders—some of article length—by Freeman. The *American Anthropologist* for December 1983 devoted a special section to the controversy, including an introduction by Ivan Brady and comments by four anthropologists followed by a satirical piece treating Freeman's work as a melodrama. *Canberra Anthropology* similarly published a special issue devoted to the debate including the comments of seven anthropologists and a detailed retort by Freeman (1983b). The *American Anthropolo-*

gist published a further review article five years later (1988).

Various reviewers note that Freeman often seizes upon Mead's most categorical generalizations even when these are at odds with other more qualified ones. They perceptively remind us that the more agonistic Samoa that Freeman emphasizes is not inconsistent with the "kinder, gentler" Samoa stressed by Mead; clearly, Samoans like the rest of us may sometimes display one characteristic and sometimes the other. But, in fairness to Freeman, he seems himself to acknowledge this; his emphasis is simply intended to counter Mead's overly Arcadian emphasis. A host of other subtle and valuable points are made by various reviewers some of which we shall attend to later. However, many of the reviewers, whatever their perspective on the substance of the controversy, were put off by what they regarded as a hostile and contentious tone in Freeman's "refutation."

After so much review, it may be asked why there is need to say more. First, none of the reviews is based on an examination of Mead's field materials, so the authors were not in a position to know what she had observed. Second, my analysis is based on a perspective very different from what is currently fashionable in anthropology. To put it indelicately, few of the reviewers accept the ordinary scientific requirement that propositions must in principle be verifiable and should be accepted or rejected by consideration of their fit with observations.

From the outset, most cultural anthropologists have practiced the discipline as though unaware of the requirement of verifiability. A few brave souls have tried to bring the discipline around and have produced a small corpus of works that meet the requirements of science. These works, however, seldom pretend to provide answers that definitively support one side or the other in the great ideological disputes of the time; they are therefore likely to be appreciated only by a tiny band willing to settle for ordinary empirical understanding. Most of this work is confined to cognitive anthropology, linguistics, and, occasionally, economic anthropology. It often requires some technical competence and facility with logical and mathematical tools and is therefore inaccessible to many in the profession, not to speak of the general reading public. If the pioneers in cultural anthropology were in practice unscientific, many of the leading lights among contemporary anthropologists practice an anthropology that is avowedly nonempirical on the grounds that verifiability is inappropriate to the investigation of human behavior.

The requirement of verifiability is considered by these anthropologists to be a manifestation of "positivism," which they regard as outmoded. The most extreme position within this camp is that all understanding is a "construction" devised to serve interests quite independent of knowing the truth; indeed, these extremists would scoff at the notion of "truth" as anything other than a perspective related to one's position in society or in space. This they think is consistent with the relativistic findings of modern physics. Freed from the constraints of empirical verification, many of these anthropologists speak a language almost totally unintelligible to those of us who are looking for empirical referents and relational terms whose meanings we clearly grasp. It is a kind of speaking in tongues perhaps emulative of certain French savants of great erudition but no understanding of science. It is from this perspective that many of the reviews of the Mead-Freeman debate were written. My perspective is so profoundly different as to require yet another look at the controversy.

We might do well to begin by acknowledging that certain of Freeman's criticisms are wellfounded; certainly there has been a long-standing bias against including biological factors in our understanding of human behavior, and a number of Mead's statements regarding life in Samoa are very misleading. In addition, Freeman should be credited with presentation of considerable valuable historical and cultural-behavioral data relevant to the problems that Mead raises. Methodologically, however, he is part of the problem. Though, happily, he does not speak in tongues as is the current fashion, he is himself a victim of the time-honored unscientific perspective and practice of cultural anthropology. Entirely unaware of how profoundly unscientific Mead's work is, he imagines that he can "refute" assertions that are so vague as to be "not even wrong." Beyond this, much of his criticism is directed at the afterimage of Mead's work rather than at what she actually said. Nevertheless, his courageous challenge raises the question how a work that is so misleading could have remained so popular for so long. Surely there is something wrong with cultural anthropology if this is the case. Freeman therefore provides us with an opportunity to examine the defects of our discipline. Rather than responding like political "spin doctors" seeking to minimize the damage to our reputation, it would be far better to attack the causes of our failure.

Freeman's explanation of the Mead's success is that the field was so eager to demonstrate the power of culture vis-à-vis biology that it uncritically accepted her claims. What he seems not to see, however, is that if the bias had been the opposite—in favor of the more interactive biology and culture that he advocates—the problems with her work would have remained, only with a different slant. Mead's failures were partly those of cultural anthropology then and now; she did not make her claims clear enough to be tested and she did not present sufficient or adequately representative data to support her generalizations. Had she met these requirements of ordinary scientific practice, whatever her predilections regarding culture and biology, she could not without falsifying observations have written the rather misleading account that she did.

Moreover, Mead knew perfectly well that the sex life of female adolescents in Samoa was by both precept and practice more restricted than what she required to make her case and more restricted than her generalizations imply. Regarding the agonistic aspects of Samoan life, it is evident both from what she wrote and what she chose not to report that she knew of them; needing a halcyon Samoa to make her case, she again produced misleading generalizations. In short, Mead's misleading generalizations were not the considered opinions of one who had engaged in a voyage of discovery but the polemical claims of one anxious to make a case.

The greatest fault, however, lies with those of us like myself who understood the requirements of science but both failed to point out the deficiencies of Mead's work and tacitly supported such enterprise by repeatedly assigning it to students. Had the book been similarly unscientific but with an opposite ideology, we no doubt would have ripped it apart for its scientific failings. Ideology's power to blind us persists, and its distortions are not confined to those who practice the "unnatural" sciences like cultural anthropology but also manifest among the practitioners of the more "natural" ones.

Mead sought to make her Samoan account a test case for the power of culture, whereas Freeman has presented his findings as consistent with a larger role for biology. In order to evaluate the evidence presented by Freeman, one must bear in mind that the Samoans themselves have an interest in the controversy that goes beyond getting things right. They are, naturally enough, concerned about their image. I discovered this interest before Freeman's book had appeared while I was doing fieldwork in a village in Western Samoa, far from Manu'a where Mead did her work but in a village adjacent to the one in which Freeman had worked. One in a group of men who regularly gathered in the village was missing when I came upon them; this man was the butt of numerous jokes regarding his manhood, and when I asked where he was, I was told that he had read Mead and had gone to do *moetotolo* (surreptitious rape conducted at night while a woman is sleeping) because Mead said that it was acceptable to do so! At this everyone laughed, and I was astonished because I had no idea that anyone in the village was even aware of Mead. Certainly no resident of the village knew English well enough to read Mead with any real understanding, but on inquiry I found that many in the village and throughout Samoa knew of her existence. She was widely believed to have depicted Samoa as sexually promiscuous and thereby impugned Samoan dignity. It is highly probable that this view originated with a few sophisticated Samoans some of whom had actually read Mead and had spread throughout Samoa by the grapevine that the Samoans refer to as *ūalesi moso'oi* (the liana wireless). There is no question, then, that most Samoans would welcome Freeman's claim that Mead greatly exaggerated Samoan sexual promiscuity, though at least one Samoan wag has claimed that Mead's depiction has served him well by increasing his chances of exploits among white women. What is important to keep in mind, then, is that like the anthropologists and those with an ideological stake in the findings, the Samoans are not simply disinterested observers, since in their view their image is at stake.

Those who have closely followed the Mead-Freeman controversy will know—and others should know—that in the heat of battle a great many lively tidbits have been presented concerning the character, behavior, and mental condition of Mead and Freeman. Some of this information has been offered under the dubious cover that it is relevant to the reliability of each of them. Though I have been privy to much of this information through informal sources as well as in published critiques, I have found it irrelevant to understanding the controversy and have refrained from discussing any such "revelations." I must, however, say a word about myself. I am an anthropologist who has done some fieldwork in Western Samoa, spending a total of a year and a half there in the 1970s and '80s. My fieldwork had only the most marginal connection with the issues raised by the Mead-Freeman controversy, having to do primarily with economics and social organization and the quality of life of different segments of the population. I can speak and understand a little Samoan, though very imperfectly, and therefore I had every lengthy field-material document in Mead's collection translated by a native speaker, with whom I went over each sentence. I similarly relied on a translator for every handwritten document in Samoan, of whatever length, because even in English it is often difficult to read Mead's handwriting.

Though I heard Mead give addresses on numerous occasions and once joined a small luncheon gathering that she attended and even spoke a few words to her, I did not know her in a personal way. I became acquainted with Derek Freeman only recently. Since by chance my fieldwork was carried out in the village adjacent to the one in which he worked, I first learned of him during a visit to this village, where the villagers uniformly praised his knowledge of their customs (*aganu'u*) and his mastery of the Samoan language. Other Samoans who knew him confirmed his knowledge and skill. My contact with him began after he got wind of my examination of Mead's field materials and initiated a correspondence with me. In 1990 he mentioned to me in a letter that he would be in California, and I invited him to give two lectures at my university (University of California, Riverside) on April 5 and 6, 1990. During the period of his lectures he stayed at my house, and we had ample opportunity to discuss things Samoan and other matters of mutual interest. Like others of whatever persuasion regarding the Mead-Freeman dispute, I was impressed with his extensive knowledge of Samoa. We have since carried out a lengthy correspondence. After examining a first draft of this book he offered numerous criticisms, and on certain factual matters I found his criticism to be correct and altered my account accordingly. I remain grateful to him for these corrections. On a number of larger issues we remain sharply divided. Perhaps it is fair to say that our outlooks are so profoundly different that, as Winston Churchill said of Americans and the English, we are divided by a common language.

I must also confess that from the time of my first fieldwork in Samoa I had had a number of experiences that seemed to me somewhat discrepant with what I remembered of Mead's depiction of Samoa. While my family and I were in Hawaii on the way to the field, my then-adolescent daughter was warned by knowledgeable Samoans about the danger of rape, a practice that Mead, to my recollection, had said was most un-Samoan. Having arrived in Western Samoa, in seeking advice about where I might best carry on my work I was surprised to find a number of villages being ruled out on the grounds that they were plagued with discord and even violence. Certainly by the end of my first year of fieldwork in Samoa I had the impression that the Samoa I had seen was far more agonistic than Mead had depicted it. These impressions of mine certainly contributed to my desire to examine what Mead had actually observed and to reexamine what she had said. It is a wise person indeed who is fully aware of his own bias and a fool who thinks he has none. As for myself, I am aware of but one bias that I should report: I am hopeful that, after so much has been said on the Mead-Freeman dispute, I have found something worthwhile to add. I have tried not to bend with the wind, but it would be too much to hope that I have not been bent.

Notes, Introduction

1. All citations from *Coming of Age in Samoa* are from the William Morrow 1973 edition.

2. The proper Samoan rendering of "Samoa" requires a macron over the first "a," but I shall omit it throughout the text and follow the ordinary English usage.

3. This point is nicely made by Feinberg (1988:656), who says in his review article that he "will try to highlight what Mead actually said, pointing up the notable discrepancy between the popular perception and her actual account."

1

The Fieldwork

The nine inhabited islands constituting Samoa lie in the South Pacific between 13° and 14° south latitude and 168° and 173° longitude west. Politically they are divided between American Samoa and Western Samoa. At the time of Mead's study, American Samoa was under the jurisdiction of the Department of the Navy; in 1951 authority was transferred to the Department of the Interior.[1] The inhabited islands of American Samoa are Tutuila, with its port of Pago Pago, Aunu'u, Ofu, Olosega, and Ta'ū. Though Mead spent more than two months on Tutuila, most of her fieldwork was done on Ta'ū. This island and Ofu and Olosega are known as the Manu'a group. On Ta'ū there is a village of Ta'ū, which even at the time of Mead's study was politically divided into two sections, Lumā and Si'ufaga. Mead's most extensive fieldwork was conducted in both sections of Ta'ū and in the adjacent village to the northeast, Faleāsao.

The Field Materials*

It is to Mead's everlasting credit that she preserved her field materials so that they may be examined for scholarly

---

*Quotes from Margaret Mead's field materials are courtesy of The Institute for Intercultural Studies, Inc. (New York City). The field materials are presented verbatim, with misspellings left uncorrected.

purposes. Many anthropologists have confessed to me that they would never have had the courage to do so; the conjecture must surely be that these anthropologists have claimed more than was warranted by their observations. I was required to obtain the permission of Mead's daughter, Catherine Bateson, herself a distinguished anthropologist, to examine the field materials. I gladly gave her my word that I would protect the anonymity of Mead's subjects; I have therefore omitted all real names of such persons from this book.

Mary Wolfskill of the Library of Congress Manuscript Division, who has thoughtfully organized the materials, gave me patient guidance in their use. For purposes of reference I have divided the field materials into seven categories; (1) binder, fifty handwritten pages almost entirely in English containing most of the data regarding specific girls in her study; (2) fieldnotes, handwritten but occasionally copied on the typewriter, sometimes in Samoan, on subjects ranging from food preparation to sexuality; (3) news bulletins, typed and apparently sent back to the United States to be distributed to certain relatives and friends, beginning on August 10, 1925, her last day at sea before reaching Hawaii, and ending on March 24, 1926, about a month and a half before leaving American Samoa, and containing personal impressions and accounts of particular experiences; (4) letters to Samoans she had met during her fieldwork and from them to her (those from Samoans and one of hers in Samoan) and letters to and from Franz Boas and to other acquaintances; (5) a census of the three villages on Ta'ū in which she worked; (6) tables relating to census data and to pseudonyms she had attached to various people; and (7) psychological data, notes on the psychological tests of intelligence that she administered and their results.

From these field materials, it is possible to assemble some precise and some approximate dates connected with significant events in Mead's field experience.

The Itinerary

She arrived on Tutuila in American Samoa on August 31, 1925, and remained there for a little more than two months. She departed for Ta'ū on November 9, 1925. On March 8, 1926, she visited the nearby islands of Ofu and Olosega, where she stayed for ten days. She then returned to Ta'ū, where she remained for about five months, until approximately April 16, 1926. From Ta'ū she returned to Tutuila and probably left Samoa on May 10, 1926. Her total field trip was about eight months long.

While staying on Tutuila she had a number of experiences that were important to her understanding of Samoan life, and her accounts of these experiences suggest something of her predispositions and point of view.

Some of her more important experiences on Tutuila are listed below in chronological order:

September 1. She went to the Missionary Rest Home where she met and interviewed Miss Holder, head of the Atauloma girls school.

October 1. She attended the trial in Pago Pago of a fifteen-year-old girl who had bitten off another's ear and another trial involving charges of bigamy.

October 3. The Mormons found her an excellent informant who held an important position in the town of Pago Pago on Tutuila.

October 10. She went to the village of Leone on Tutuila and met a "half-caste" Samoan woman, her Samoan mother, and her nephew. That evening she went palolo fishing. (The palolo is a sea annelid.)

About October 19–October 28. She spent time in Vaitogi, a village on Tutuila, with the high chief Ufuti and his family, with whom she remained in contact by mail throughout her stay in Samoa. Here she received the *tāupou* title Sinaualo. (*Tāupou* = holder of title given to virgins honored for elegance of appearance and manners.)[2]

For Mead's stay in Ta'ū, a few key dates are as follows:

November 9. She arrived in Ta'ū and moved in with the Holt family. Mr. Holt was a chief pharmacist's mate and administered a medical dispensary under the authority of the Navy. Mead had met Mrs. Holt earlier in Tutuila, where the latter had gone to give birth to her second child. The Holts provided Mead with a room of her own, and her informants often visited her at their home.

January 1. There was a damaging and frightening hurricane, followed ten days later by a severe storm.

January 26. The mother of the high chief Tufele bestowed upon Mead her second *tāupou* title. Plans were made to visit the village of Fitiuta, on the opposite end of the island, this being Tufele's home village.

During the week beginning February 7th, made what was probably a one day visit to the village of Amouli near the southwestern tip of the island.

February 20–March 3. She went with Tufele, his mother, and an entourage to Fitiuta. They were accompanied on this trip by the Cooke expedition from the Bishop Museum of Hawaii. Here she spent several days and received another *tāupou* title, Iligagoa.

March 8–March 17. She spent time on the islands of Ofu and Olosega.

Language

Mead came to Samoa with no knowledge of the language, and Freeman argues that "imperfect command" was the most that she ever attained. As early as 1972 he noted 214 spelling errors of Samoan words in a new edition of Mead's *Social Organization of Manu'a* (Freeman 1972). Though a number of these errors involve the use of the macron, which the Samoans themselves frequently omit, many are vowel errors typically difficult for English-speakers; often these vowel errors lead to

confusion of words that are otherwise similar. We know from
her own account that she began studying Samoan less than
a week after her arrival on Tutuila. Her teacher was a Samoan
nurse who, we are told, was of "chiefly family a cousin to
Tufeli" (Tufele). Mead continued to misspell the name of
Tufele, an important chief and informant who lived in
Manu'a, where her fieldwork was performed until March 22,
1926. When she reached Manu'a on November 9, she had
had a little over two months of Samoan study. In a
newsbulletin written in March she refers to the island of
"Olesega," indicating that her vowel recognition was no better
for islands than for chiefs four months into her Manu'an
fieldwork.

On December 20, 1925, about a month and a half after
her arrival in Manu'a, she wrote a letter in Samoan to the
high chief Ufuti at Vaitogi explaining that the wife of a certain
Manu'an chief spoke English quite well; she goes on to say,
"I am trying very hard to learn the Samoan language. I know
a lot of words now but there are even more that I do not
know yet." We do not know if she was helped in writing the
letter. The psychological tests that she administered were
translated into Samoan by someone else, as is indicated by
the handwriting and the existence of a presumably prior
English version. At the same time, there are numerous
fieldnotes transcribed by Mead in Samoan, one of these on
November 13, 1925. It is titled "O le Amio o le teine kerisiano"
(The Conduct of a Christian Girl); under the typed Samoan
Mead has written an English translation.

As in the *Social Organization of Manu'a*, there are numerous
Samoan-language errors in the field materials. Some may
simply be careless omissions, but others plainly indicate the
limitations of her knowledge: afa for sennit ('*afa*; without the
glottal stop it could mean a kind of tree); fatefea for
banishment (*fa'ate'a*); fa'amaiseao for defloration
(*fa'amāsei'au*); va'afauta'u for mediums (*va'afa'atau*); tafou for
roaming about (*tafao*), also spelled on the same day tafau;
tuipapepae (for knocking down the raised stone platform at

the base of a house (*tu'ipaepae*); the names Ta'aga (Toaga), Va (Vao); and Siualoao (Siaoloau); silipusi for fishing stick (*selepusi*; *sele* = snare; *pusi* = moray eel); vanna for sea urchin (*vana*); lole for sea cucumber (*loli*; *lole* = candy). As noted earlier, in *CA* Mead uniformly misspells tāupou as *taupo*, though it is spelled correctly in all field materials recorded while she was in Samoa.

Mead tells us in *CA* that "with a few unimportant exceptions this material was obtained in the Samoan language and not through the medium of interpreters. All of the work with individuals was done in the native language, as there were no young people on the island who spoke English" (1973:262). Had this been the case, Mead's language limitation might have contributed substantially to misunderstanding. However, her own listing of thirty female adolescents notes that one spoke "quite good English," four "good," two "fair," and two "little." The field materials indicate also that a number of adults of both sexes, as well as a number of male youths, spoke English.

The binder, which contains most of the material on adolescents, is almost entirely in English, with a word or two of Samoan in various places. For example, in a note of February 16, 1926, we read that a twenty-two-year-old male "says it is sa to usu le gafa [forbidden to recite a genealogy] if anyone but the family is around." Following this there is a statement completely in English about a twenty-one-year-old woman who "says married when 15 against her will." Since the binder contains most of the material on adolescent girls and is supplemented by tables and occasional notes in newsbulletins, also overwhelmingly in English, it follows that virtually all the data on adolescent girls are transcribed in English. How they were obtained we cannot ascertain, but it is noteworthy that data contained in the fieldnotes were often transcribed by Mead in Samoan and invariably as dictated by some informant. For example, the woman who served as her servant, who spoke no English, provided Mead with an account of a Christian girl's conduct and the conduct of a sister. A young man from Vaitogi told her about brother-sister taboos. Someone dictated a model love letter to her. A *matai* (titled person) from Vaitogi told her the story of the turtle and the shark. A ten-year-old female wrote out a dream that she had had. It would seem, then, that the largely English-language transcription in the binder indicates that much of the information about adolescents was obtained from English speaking informants using English to communicate. Examples from the field materials indicate that such largely English conversation with adolescents and other young people did take place. No such conversations in Samoan are recorded in any of the field materials, nor are there any accounts of events regarding adolescents recorded in Samoan.

Numbers

Mead tells us that her study "included sixty-eight[3] girls between the ages of eight and nine and nineteen or twenty—all the girls between these ages in the three villages of Faleāsao, Lumā and Siufaga, the three villages on the west coast of the island of Ta'ū in the Manu'a Archipelago of the Samoan Islands" (1973:282). The age spread of "eight and nine" and "nineteen or twenty" is, as she explains, due to the "impossibility of obtaining accurate dates of birth except in a very few cases" (282). That she considered "all the girls between these ages in the three villages," however, is not at all in accord with her census data. All the girls between these ages might be taken to include those equal to or greater than eight and equal to or less than twenty, of which the census includes 110. This age spread seems the most sensible interpretation of her wording and also is in accord with the actual age-range of the subjects covered. However, even if one were to exclude those of eight and those of twenty, the total would be 98. There is, therefore, a maximum discrepancy of 42, and a minimum discrepancy of 30.

Perhaps it is noteworthy that in none of her works on Samoa does Mead supply the basic census data that she obtained—total population of the three villages, sex and age distribution, and the like. The closest that she comes to providing such summary census data is her statement in *CA* that "the writer therefore chose to work in one small locality, in a group numbering only six hundred people" (1973:260). Obviously, 600 is a round number, and one might guess that it was merely an approximation, though it is surprising where a census exists that one would not provide these findings. Even more surprising is that the total population provided by counting all persons listed in her unpublished census is 785, a discrepancy of 185.[4] To account for this discrepancy one might surmise that 600 is an estimate of the population of the two neighboring villages of Lumā and Si'ufaga and excludes the population of Faleāsao. The population of these two aforementioned villages is 555 according to Mead's census. Perhaps the key words justifying the 600 figure are "chose to work in one small locality." The joint community of Lumā and Si'ufaga is indeed where Mead resided and did most of her work. (However, the sample of girls came also from Faleāsao.) In a letter to Boas of November 29, 1925, Mead says that the villages of Lumā and Si'ufaga "between them have 580 inhabitants." She then adds that Faleasau has a population of 259; thus the total population would be 839. The exact total population is not significant in evaluating Mead's evidence, but the wobbling reports of this population are consistent with the general unreliability of numerical evidence throughout *CA*. Moreover, some of the demographic inconsistencies regarding the girls being studied are indeed relevant in evaluating her findings.

In Appendix I (1973:251–253), nine of those listed as adolescent are not found in the census; two of those "just reaching puberty" and two of those listed as "pre-adolescents" are also not in the census. Perfection is not for this world, but perhaps we may conclude that at least these additional thirteen persons should be added to the census? There is further evidence from the list she calls "Key Numbers" that the community includes other persons beyond those already noted. Clearly, there were considerably more young people between the ages of eight and nine and nineteen or twenty than Mead indicates. A certain carelessness about these matters is also evident, and it is repeated in numerous other instances.

For the twenty-five adolescents listed in Mead's Appendix V, Table I (1973:285), the true names are provided in every case but one. These names with but one exception are found in the census, and except in one instance each is found in the household indicated.[5] The clear exception involves an individual living not simply in a different house but in a different village. Perhaps this is one of the many cases of the residence shifting that Mead argues is prevalent. Of those just reaching puberty, thirteen living in Lumā and Si'ufaga are listed in Appendix I, and the true names are provided again in every case but one (285). All of these named girls are found in the census. Again, the houses indicated in the Appendix are essentially correct; in one instance a girl lives three houses away from the listed house and in two other cases in an adjacent house. In the case of the preadolescents, who were of course less relevant to Mead's inquiry, no fictitious names are provided for Faleāsao; however, such names are provided for twelve of the nineteen preadolescents living in Lumā and Si'ufaga. Three of these are not found in the census, and of the nine that are in the census one is found in a different village and household than indicated.

Clearly, the pseudonymous list of girls in Appendix I corresponds quite closely to real census data. In view of the previous inaccuracy, we are not surprised to learn that the number of girls in Appendix I is seventy-two rather than the sixty-eight said to be the total in Appendix V. Because this seventy-two is considerably less than the number in the census, it is obviously impossible that the number of girls within the relevant age-range in the Appendix exactly corresponds to the number in the census. Because the number of children in a household is important to Mead, it is worthy of note that the number per household is generally in correspondence with the census. Of the fifty-one households cited as having female children of the relevant age and developmental categories in the Appendix, only eleven have a different number of these children in the census; ten of these have one more relevant child and one has three additional children. The large total difference between the Appendix and the census stems chiefly from the fact that many houses in the census have relevant children not cited in the Appendix.

A hasty reading might suggest that the adolescents and those just reaching puberty from Appendix I would be identical or nearly so to those found in Appendix V, especially since the totals are identical. In fact four of the names of adolescents in Appendix I are not included in Appendix V, and five of the names in Appendix V are not found in Appendix I. (There are two Litas in Appendix I and one Lita in Appendix V, two Tulipas in Appendix V and one Tulipa in Appendix I.) Furthermore, one of those listed as an adolescent in Appendix V (Aso [Table I], or Iso [Table II], an obvious typo) is listed as having just reached puberty in Appendix I. Similarly, five of those listed in Appendix I as having just reached puberty are not found in Appendix V under "midways," and five of those included in Appendix V as "midways" are not found in Appendix I under those having just reached puberty. One of those listed in this category in Appendix I (Aso) is listed as an adolescent in Appendix V.

In two places Mead speaks of the number of girls "studied in detail." In Appendix II (1973:261) she says that twenty-eight "children who as yet showed no signs of puberty (pre-ads)," fourteen "children who would probably mature within the next year or year and a half" (midways) and twenty-five "girls who had passed puberty within the last four years but were not yet classed by the community as adults (adolescents) *were studied in detail*" (my italics). Thus sixty-seven children are said to have been studied in detail. However, in Appendix V Mead again speaks of the same three age categories of girls providing the same numbers, but this time she says that "eleven of the younger children were studied in detail, making a group of fifty. The remaining fourteen children in the youngest group were studied less carefully as individuals." Clearly the meaning of "studied in detail" has changed from one Appendix to another. Perhaps Mead's final operative definition of "studied in detail" refers to having obtained all the family structure data provided in Table II of Appendix V (286–87), for this table precisely provides the same fifty girls noted above. For the adolescents, "studied in detail" probably means having obtained data on "time elapsed since puberty, periodicity (frequency of menses), pain, masturbation, homosexual experience, [and] residence in Pastor's household," all of which appear in Table I, Appendix V (285).

We should finally note that the listing of different individuals in Appendix I and Appendix V need not be regarded as an error because those in Appendix I include all the girls mentioned in the chapter "The Girl and Her Age Group" (1973:59–73) in *CA*, whereas those in Appendix V are girls "studied in detail."

Notes, Chapter 1, The Fieldwork

1. Western Samoa in the 1920s was governed by New Zealand under a mandate of the League of Nations and gained its independence in 1962.

2. Throughout *CA* Mead misspells *tāupou* as *taupo*, though it is spelled correctly in the field materials.

3. Though Mead says (*CA*, Appendix V) the total is sixty-eight, the subcategories of pre-ads (twenty-eight), midways (fourteen), and ads (twenty-five) total sixty-seven.

4. Because of the movement of people who are listed more than once and various doubtful entries and omissions, this number is certainly not to be taken as precise; however, the ambiguities are far too few to account for the discrepancies cited.

5. Two individuals are assigned to a neighboring house, but considering normal Samoan patterns of housing in which closely connected family members often live adjacently, they may well represent shifts from one house to another.

2

The Argument

Mead's starting point is that adolescence in the United States in the 1920s was indeed a difficult period marked by such features as "rebellion against authority, philosophical perplexities, the flowering of idealism, conflict and struggle" (1973:5). These difficulties of adolescence were "documented in the records of schools and juvenile courts" (4). Whether this impressionistic characterization is correct is not a point of contention. What Mead contests is that these characteristics are due to "the physical changes which are going on in the bodies of your boys and girls" (3). Her hunch, derived from anthropological wisdom regarding the plasticity of human nature, is that they are more likely the result of the social environment than of a biological condition.

Mead's argument is that if she can find one human society in which adolescence lacks the characteristics noted for adolescence in the United States, then it will follow that they are not the inevitable products of biology but the result of social conditions. Such an inquiry might contribute to an understanding of what these social conditions are by contrasting the conditions obtaining in the two cases. An unstated presupposition of this argument is that whatever biological differences there might be between the two contrasted societies, they would be irrelevant to the behavioral and experiential differences encountered.

Strictly speaking, the argument requires a society in which adolescence is less stressful than the United States but also one in which adolescence is at least no more stressful than other stages of life; were adolescence found to be less stressful than in the United States but more than other stages of life, it could still be argued that biology was exercising some influence. Although Mead does provide some information relevant to stress at different stages of life in Samoa, she does not attend to its relevance. There is a possible ambiguity in the argument as to whether biological determination simply means that adolescence will be stressful or whether it implies such specific effects as flowering idealism and philosophical perplexities. Mead claims theses specific effects as well as stress are relevant to the argument and emphasizes these effects in expressing her doubt about biological determination.

Mead presents a number of anecdotal examples as well as generalizations regarding stress in Samoa, particularly among adolescent girls. However, "philosophical perplexities" receive no empirical treatment, nor is any such inquiry indicated in the field materials. Perhaps she would have argued that she simply observed no such manifestation so there was nothing to report or that it followed from theoretical considerations. The same may be said of "idealism," which also receives no explicit attention in either *CA* or the field materials.

Her general contention that life for adolescent girls in Samoa was less stressful than for American adolescent girls rests entirely on her assertion that this is her impression and that it follows from theoretical presuppositions. Clearly, the weight that should be given to her evaluation of the empirical evidence for stress depends upon a comparison of those data with some imagined U.S. data, but the idea of conducting such an assessment boggles the mind. The theoretical arguments that follow similarly require comparison with arguments pertinent to the United States and its cultural practices. What Mead provides instead is arguments in favor of a less stressful life in Samoa.

"Organization of the family and the attitude towards sex are undoubtedly the most important . . . among factors . . . influential in producing stable, well-adjusted, robust individuals" (1973:223). The "general education concept which disapproves of precocity and coddles the slow, the laggard, the inept" (223) presumably helps the "slow," while the potential boredom of the "bright" is avoided by "the slower pace dictated by the climate, the complacent, peaceful society, and the compensation of the dance," which allows the "blatant display of individuality which the bright child feels" (224). The chief contrasting characteristic of family organization that Mead thinks relevant to her argument is the generally larger size of the family residential unit. Because there are many children, the problem of the spoiled child seldom arises; many are there to share burdens, and children are generally available as companions. The diffusion of affection from a child to many adults reduces the intensity of the bond and results in a lifelong lack of intensive attachment. The individual's stakes in a given relationship is thereby lowered, thus reducing the stress in that relationship. This "seems to ensure the child against the development of the crippling attitudes which have been labelled Oedipus complexes, Electra complexes, and so on" (213).

This diffusion of affection is "further reinforced by the segregation of the boys from the girls," the child coming to regard others in terms of social categories rather than in terms of their "individuality" (1973:210). "All claim of personal attraction or congeniality between relatives of opposite sex must be flouted. All of this means that casual sex relations carry no onus of strong attachment, that the marriage of convenience dictated by economic and social consideration is easily borne and casually broken without strong emotion" (210).[1]

Alleged diffusion of affection links with lack of specialization of feeling, particularly sexual feeling (1973:215), makes marital adjustment easy and results in lack of frigidity and psychic impotence. In addition, sex knowledge is widespread ("ten-year olds are . . . sophisticated, although they witness sex activities only surreptitiously" [134]), familiarity and teaching producing "a scheme of personal relations in which there were no neurotic pictures, no frigidity, no impotence," and great capacity (151). Because sex is regarded as natural, "no Puritan self-accusations vexed their consciences" (242); "minor sex activities, suggestive dancing, stimulating salacious conversation, salacious songs and definitely motivated tussling are all acceptable and attractive diversion" (148), and there is a similar playful attitude toward homosexuality. Lacking "secrecy, ignorance, guilty knowledge, faulty speculations" and understanding the "accompanying excitement" of sex as well as the bare facts, Samoans are said to be much better-adjusted than Americans (216). (All of these benefits claimed for Samoan sexual understanding and practice would seem to be advantages for all ages and both sexes; perhaps a case could be made that they are particularly relevant to adolescents who are just entering the adult sexual arena.) "So, high up in our list of explanations [of lack of stress in Samoan life] we must place the lack of deep feeling which the Samoans have conventionalised until it is the very framework of all their attitudes toward life" (200).

Judging by the language used, another Samoan advantage of great importance is apparently the comparative homogeneity of their culture, for Mead says that "the principal causes of our adolescent's difficulty are the presence of conflicting standards and the belief that every individual should make his or her own choices, coupled with a feeling that choice is an important matter" (234–35). In addition to these major factors resulting in less stress, Mead cites a number of lesser factors, including slow change, no economic cycle, tolerance of difference, no implacable God, low stakes in enterprise, an acceptable standard of living and an absence of great disasters, and the ability of adolescent girls to turn over childcare and household drudgery to young siblings and to move about from their natal homes to those of other relatives to escape from painful family situations.

Having examined the argument, we are in a position to look at the evidence available to us in *CA* and in the field materials to see what weight we should give to it and to what degree it substantiates Mead's case. We shall of course give particular attention to the evidence bearing on factual claims disputed by Freeman.

Notes, Chapter 2, The Argument

1. Whatever one may think of these alleged consequences of a large family, one must note the subtle switch here from a language of behavioral fact (large family and segregation of the sexes, with concomitant understanding and affect) to one of obligation ("must be flouted"). The notion of obligation seems inconsistent with the suggestion that the individual is preadapted to be unconcerned with personal attachment. Perhaps Mead meant both an obligation and a preadaptation.

3

Adolescent Sexuality: "Just the Facts"

This first of two chapters on sexuality presents data the from the field materials and compares it point for point with the text in CA. The following chapter provides an assessment and evaluation of this material. If this examination of Mead's work points to any lesson, it is how closely one must attend to the data in evaluating conclusions.

A table in Mead's field materials records data relevant to the sexual experience of twenty-five postmenarcheal girls: time since first period, periodicity, pain, masturbation, homosexual experience, heterosexual experience, and residence in the household of the pastor (*faife'au*), this last being relevant because it is contingent on chastity. A table with the same items is contained in *CA* (Appendix V, Table I). My table 1 presents the data from the field materials and, below each entry, the matching data from the book.

Table 1

Female Sexual Data from Field Materials and
Corresponding Data from *Coming of Age in Samoa*

Name	Pseudonym	Time since First Menstruation[a]	Periodicity[b]	Pain[c]	Masturbation	Age	Homosexual	Heterosexual	Residence with Pastor
1	Loia	2 mos.	mo.	b	+	?	+	-	+
		2 mos.	mo.	b	+		+	-	+
2	Tulipa	2 mos.	mo.	a, b	+	15		-	+
		2 mos.	mo.	a, b	+		+	-	+
3	Mala	2 mos.	mo.	b	+	19	-	-	-
		2 mos.	mo.	b	+		-	-	-
4	Leta	2 mos.	mo.	ext	+	15	-	-	+
		2 mos.	mo.	none	+		+	+	+
5	Lua	3 mos.	mo.	b	+	15	-	-	-
		3 mos.	mo.	b	-		-	-	-
6	Tolo	3 mos.	2/mo.	none	+	17	-	-	-
		3 mos.	2/mo.	ext	+		-	-	-
7	Pala	6 mos.	mo.	none	+	14	-	-	-
		6 mos.	mo.	none	+		+	-	-
8	Fala[d]	?	?	?	?	16, 17	?	?	?
		1 yr.	mo.	b	+	?	+	+	-
9	Lola	1 yr.	2/mo.	a,b	+	17	+	+	left
		1 yr.	2/mo.	a	+		+	+	-
10	Aso	1.5 yr.	2/mo.	b	+	15	+	-	?
		1.5 yr.	2/mo.	b	+		-	-	-
11	Losa	2 yrs.	mo.	a,b	-	14	+	-	+
		2 yrs.	mo.	a,b	-		+	-	+
12	Lita	2 yrs.	mo.	b	+	14, 15	+	-	+
		2 yrs.	mo.	b	+		+	-	-
13	Ana	2 yrs.	2/mo.	b	-	19	+	-	+
		2 yrs.	3 mos.	b	+		+	-	+
14	Ela	2 yrs.	mo.	ext	+	15	+	+	+
		2 yrs.	mo.	ext	+		+	+	+
15	Luna	3 yrs.	mo.	a	+	18	+	+	-
		3 yrs.	mo.	a	+		+	+	-
16	Masina	3 yrs.	mo.	a	+	19	+	+	-
		3 yrs.	mo.	a	+		+	+	-

Name	Pseudonym	Time since First Menstruation[a]	Periodicity[b]	Pain[c]	Masturbation	Age	Homosexual	Heterosexual	Residence with Pastor
17	Sona	3 yrs.	2/mo.	a,b	+	15	+	-	+
		3 yrs.	2/mo.	a,b	+		+	-	+
18	Lotu	3 yrs.	mo.	ext	+	17	+	+	-
		3 yrs.	mo.	ext	+		+	+	-
19	Namu	3 yrs.	mo.	b	+	18	+	+	-
		3 yrs.	mo.	b	+		+	+	-
20	Tulipa	3 yrs.	mo.	none	+	19	+	+	-
		3 yrs.	mo.	b	+		+	+	-
21	Sala	3 yrs.	2/mo.	ext	+	17	-	+	-
		3 yrs.	2/mo.	ext	+		-	+	-
22	Tolu	4 yrs.	2/mo.	?,b	+	18	+	+	-
		4 yrs.	2/mo.	b	+		+	+	-
23	Moana	4 yrs.	?	a,b	+	15	-	+	-
		4 yrs.	2 mos.	a,b	+		-	+	-
24	Luina	4 yrs.	mo.	ext	-	17	-	-	+
		4 yrs.	mo.	ext	-		-	-	+
25	Mina	5 yrs.	mo.	ext	-	20	-	-	+
		5 yrs.	mo.	ext	-		-	-	+

Note: Subject number 1 on the fieldnote table has a pseudonym but that pseudonym does not appear in *CA*'s Table I; however, the pseudonym Loto in Table I (not listed in the "Key to Namechanges" in the field materials) provides the same data as subject 1. Fala in *CA*'s Table I has a known real name, but it is not found in the fieldnote table.

[a] *mos.*, months; *yr(s).*, years(s).
[b] *mo.*, monthly; *mos.*, months.
[c] *a*, abdomen; *b*, back; *ext*, extreme.
[d] Absent from fieldnote table.

Though all the percentages of sexual activity are a little higher in *CA*'s Table I, clearly the figures are close and the discrepancies few. There are three discrepancies regarding masturbation, four regarding homosexuality, one regarding heterosexuality, and one regarding residence with the pastor.

	Masturbation	Homosexuality	Heterosexuality	Res. with Pastor
Field Note Table	20/24=83%	14/24=58%	10/24=42%	10/23=43%
Table I	21/25=85%	17/25=68%	12/25=48%	9/25=36%

For one of the three discrepancies (subject 23) regarding masturbation there is information in the binder: "Doesn't m—and believes it is [?]¹ the practice of the married." Apparently this is simply an error of transcription. There are no relevant data on the homosexual discrepancies. The one discrepancy regarding heterosexuality (subject 4) can probably be resolved by the following entry in the binder: "raped age 8; only case rape in Tau. There is another in Olosega." Perhaps this was not counted as heterosexual experience in the fieldnote table but was so counted in the book.

Data on one additional girl who is not postmenarcheal might also be considered relevant, and Mead herself includes her as an adolescent in fieldnote charts. Of this girl (age sixteen) she notes: "Only example of pre-pubertal sex relationship, a little [?]sophisticated flirt—probably deferred menstruation. Her aunt is [?]helpless before her preferences for tafauing." "Tafauing" is an anglicized form coined by Mead from the Samoan word *tafao*, which means to wander about or to be idle; in this instance and elsewhere she seems to associate the term with sexual adventure, though it need not have this connotation.

In addition to information in the tables, there is a variety of field material on each of these adolescents:

Subject 1 (pseudonym Loia). This subject is said to be "scared older boys; doesn't show sexual precocity of [another subject twelve years of age], rather undersexed" (binder). She does not appear in *CA*.

Subject 2 (pseudonym Tulipa).This subject is described in the binder as

> Un-comely, but subtly attractive. Excellent dancer. Sloe eyed. Shy. Is unselfconscious and [?]disappearing in the presence of older boys. (What does this mean?) (means she's younger than she looks—reported by younger children to tafau greatly with [two males]). [male who at the time of the study is twenty-two years old] is said to have m.t.t.d [*moetotolo* +English-ed = surreptitious-raped] her and she did not cry out. Now living f's [minister's] house. Says she likes it. Only 14 -[fifteen according

to census]—seems much older—looks old. Probably accounts for a good deal. Too young to have any real sex interests; glad to get away from pursuit. Family looks on [male of twenty-four] with some approval—so much higher rank.

CA indicates only that this subject has menstruated for just a few months, which is consistent with the data in the tables.

Subject 3 (pseudonym Mala). This subject is said in the binder to be

> [?]unembarrassed presence boys. Will marry some day & have [?]5 children. Marry a Tau boy and stay to take care of her parents. Has never seen a Cesarean pm [postmortem] but has seen many births. 4 of her sister. Has seen a still birth. Says all boys [here "masturbate" is crossed out and followed by two words which appear to be *veku velau*, meaning unknown; ordinary Samoan for masturbation is *fufu*] from babies till men—even after they are married. Says she never heard of a girl doing so. Lived in ff's school in days of former pastor. Left because [subject 8] beat her. Says she never wants to be a church m [member]. Now says she does want to be a churchmember. Condemned also for playing with boys.

The masturbation data here seem to conflict with those in both tables; there is no indication that Mead doubted her response. Consistent with the data in the binder, though considerably more expansive, the book says, "She played with boys, preferred boys' games, tied her *lavalava* like a boy. This behavior was displayed to the whole village who were vociferous in their condemnation. . . . Some of the more precocious boys of her own age were already beginning to look to her for possibilities of other forms of amusement" (1973:179–80).

Subject 4 (pseudonym Leta): As has already been noted, this subject, according to the binder, was raped at eight. She does not appear in the book.

Subject 5 (pseudonym Lua): From the binder one learns that this subject was "fearful first sex experience yet anxious for it." Consistent with the tables, the binder says that she has "been menstruating in Dec. of this year. Is allowed to

tafau but is musu [refuses]. Reason? tele tautalatiti [much too
young]. Will marry when she is matua [older]. That is when
she is 15. . . . Only wants one child." The book has little on
her sexual experience, noting only that her "first menstruation
was a few months past" (1973:144), which is consistent with
both tables and the data above.

Subject 6 (pseudonym Tolo): The data in the binder are
limited but consistent with the maturation data in the tables:
"only [?]matured after coming here in Oct. No interest boys
at all." The book indicates only that like that of a number of
others her "first menstruation was a few months past"
(1973:144).

Subject 7 (pseudonym Pala): According to the binder,
"[?]sensuous [?]inviting hoydens like [subject 7], seems very
abashed presence boys; usually leaves if they come; a virgin;
withdrawal from words, noise, boys." The book is consistent,
referring to Pala with some others as "still virgins, were a little
weary of their status and eager for amorous experience"
(1973:146).

Subject 8 (pseudonym Fala): This subject is not included in
the fieldnote table, but the binder describes her as a "sweet,
[?]round faced—jeune fille—Takes vicarious delight in [?]
[?]love affairs and has none of her own. [This last sentence
is crossed out.] . . . But has [?]lovers of her own also, but
seems to be more [?]concerned with the affairs of the older
girls. . . . Too lazy to be greatly aroused. One of the whole
lot who never came to see me until actually [?]importuned
near the last month of my [?]study." *CA* is not inconsistent
with the binder and even refers to vicarious delights. Fala is
described (1973:151–52) as one of three cousins

> who were popular with the youths of their own village. . . . The
> women of Fala's family were of easy virtue. . . . The three girls
> made common rendezvous with their lovers and their liaisons
> were frequent and gay. . . . Fala, the youngest, was content to
> let matters drift. Her lovers were friends and relatives of the
> lovers of her cousins and she was still sufficiently childlike and
> uninvolved to get almost as much enjoyment out of her cousins'

love affairs as out of her own."

Subject 9 (pseudonym Lola): The sexual experience of this subject plays a major role in the book, and there is relatively considerable data about her in the binder and even some in the fieldnotes. She is described in the binder as a "hoyden— splendid physical development. Changed residences several times. Intensely self-conscious in the presence of men—either giggling inordinately or indulging in slaps, punches, noisy repartee. Blushes, jealous, [?]violent. Other girls say she 'wants very much to sleep with a boy,' and all say 'she promenades a great deal.' The binder confirms the fieldnote table in reporting that she once "went to pastor's school."

The story told of her in *CA* (173–77) is the following:

> Lola was seventeen, a tall, splendidly developed, intelligent hoyden. She had an unusual endowment in her capacity for strong feeling, for enthusiasms, for violent responses to individuals. . . . Lola was quarrelsome, insubordinate, impertinent. . . . When she was fourteen, she became so unmanageable at home that her uncle sent her to live in the pastor's household. She stayed there through a year of stormy scenes until she was finally expelled after a fight with Mala, the other delinquent. . . . As consciousness of sex became more acute, she became slightly subdued and tentative in her manner. . . . [After some time in her uncle's household, she ran away to other relatives in the next village.] But she had only been established here about a month when another chief, with a young and beautiful *taupo* [*tāupou*] in his train, came to visit her new chief and the whole party was lodged in the very house where she slept. . . . The Don Juan of the village was a sleek, discreet man of about forty, a widower, a *matai*, a man of circumspect manner and winning ways. He was looking for a second wife and turned his attention toward the visitor. . . . But Fuativa was a cautious and calculating lover. . . . And he noticed that Lola had reached a robust girlhood and stopped to pluck this ready fruit by the way. . . . With all her capacity for violence, Lola possessed also a strong capacity for affection. Fuativa was a skilled and considerate lover. Few girls were quite so fortunate in their first lovers, and so few felt such unmixed regret when the first love affair was broken

off. Fuativa won her easily and after three weeks which were
casual to him, and very important to her, he proposed for the
hand of the visitor. . . . The rage of Lola was unbounded and
she took an immediate revenge, publicly accusing her rival of
being a thief and setting the whole village by the ears.

The binder is much thinner here than the book, but the
event of the seduction and the character and appearance of
Lola are in close correspondence: "[?]took [male with
pseudonym Fuativa] as lover. Then he proposes to [female
called "visitor" in *CA*] and [subject 9] accuses [visitor] of
being a thief in revenge." In the fieldnotes Mead has the
following colloquy with Lola: "Would you rather live in the
pastor's house or at home? Why?" (Answer) "Because there
are such a lot of nice girls there and I don't like the older
girls in our family as well." (Question) "Who decided you
should go to live there?" (Answer) "[A *matai* known as Fua
in the book]." The notation in the fieldnote table that she
had "left" the minister's residence is consistent with the
lengthy explanation in the book and her dislike of the girls
in her own family, as indicated above, corroborates the
difficulties described in there.

    Subject 10 (pseudonym Aso): The binder notes briefly that
she is "not particularly interested boys." The book has nothing
relevant.

    Subject 11 (pseudonym Losa): The binder reports "someone
from Fitiuta reputed be in love with her." The book has
nothing relevant.

    Subject 12 (pseudonym Lita): The binder reports that this
subject "says she is much too young to marry. Wants children
doesn't want marry. Musu to a husband. Says pre-marital
intercourse is leaga [bad]. Not tafao at all. Very puritanical
in the [?]matter of lessons. Goes to bed early and then
[another subject] tafaos." In the notes to chapter 11
(1973:257–58), the book says, "During six months, I saw six
girls leave the pastor's establishment for several reasons. . . .
Lita because her father ordered her home, because with the
permission of the pastor, but without consulting her family,

she went off for a three weeks' visit in another island." This may explain the discrepancy regarding residence with the pastor indicated in the tables.

Subject 13 (pseudonym Ana): The binder says only that the subject is "charming, good looking, intelligent, thoughtful." The book describes her similarly and as a church member (1973:168–69): "gave up dancing, clung closer to the group of younger girls in the pastor's school and her foster home, the neurasthenic product of a physical defect. . . . "

Subject 14 (pseudonym Ela): According to the binder this subject "lives [with] [a minister] and was [?]bounced out once for a love affair. Then forgiven and taken back. (She denies [?]this!)" Apparently Mead does not credit her denial, because the book claims that she is the only exception to the "inverse correlation between residence at home and chastity" and mentions that she "had been forgiven and taken back into the household of a pastor where workers were short" (1973:147). Elsewhere the binder says that [male name] "never went with [subject 14] and now children say is courting [subject 11]."

Subject 15 (pseudonym Luna): This subject seems to have a reputation for amorous affairs in the book, but the binder has only the cursory note that she "has a lover." (*CA* has two girls named "Luna," but the one on p. 63 is only ten and is clearly not subject 15.) She is described there as "a lazy good-natured girl, three years past puberty." According to the book (1973:152–53),

> Luna lived for several years in the pastor's household and had gone home when her stepmother left her father. . . Luna tired of the younger girls who had been her companions in the pastor's household and sought instead two young married women among her relatives. . . . She ["a girl who had deserted her husband"] and Luna were constant companions, and Luna, quite easily and inevitably took one lover, then two, then a third—all casual affairs . . . Some day she would marry and be a church member, but now: *Laititi a'u* ("I am but young"). And who was she to give up dancing.

Subject 16 (pseudonym Masina): This subject is said in the book to have had considerable amorous experience, but the binder says only that she is said by "younger children tafao greatly." *CA* (1973:119–20) says of her that she was "the most unhappy of the older girls . . . a girl about three years past puberty. Masina could not dance . . . little charm . . . shy and ill at ease. All of her five lovers had been casual, all temporary, all unimportant. . . . No one sought her hand in marriage and she would not marry until her family needed the kind of property which forms a bride price."

Subject 17 (pseudonym Sona): In the binder Mead records that this subject "says that boys don't like her because she can't tafao. Wants live all life girls, never marry, be school girl." There is a reference to her also in a news bulletin that says nothing of her love life; Mead says that she "comes in from the reef with a cut on her back which very very bad boy has given her with a great great big stone and I must needst bandage it." Mead also records in the fieldnotes that the subject had "just returned from a malaga [trip]. . . . Did you get a sweetheart? Only dear girl friends, no boy, for all the boys in that village are my brothers." Incidentally, the quaint English recorded here is apparently not translation, for Mead notes in a news bulletin that the subject "speaks good eng." The book (1973:165–67) says,

> Sona, who was two years younger than Lita [since Sona is fifteen and Lita fourteen or fifteen, the age reference is fictional] and had also lived for several years in the pastor's household, presented a very similar picture. . . . overbearing in manner. . . . ugly little stranger. . . . Her sister has no use for marriage; neither had she. . . . Sona was not a church member. . . . it was part of her scheme of life to remain a school girl as long as possible and thus fend off responsibilities.

Subject 18 (pseudonym Lotu): The binder speaks of three girls, including this subject, who were church members and adds that she and one other did not "fall" (were not discovered to have sex and therefore excluded from the congregation). However, the book mentions someone in love with the subject

(1973:55), and later (153) it is said that she was a "church member, and had attended the missionary boarding school. She had had only one accepted lover, the illegitimate son of a chief who dared not jeopardise his very slender chance of succeeding to his father's title by marrying her. Although she was transgressing, the older church members charitably closed their eyes, sympathising with her lover's family dilemma. Her only other sex experience had been with a *moetotolo*, a relative."

Subject 19 (pseudonym Namu): According to the binder this subject is said by subject 1 to "[?]be a [?]great gad about. Has been lover one [village A] boy and one [village B]. [Village A] boy brought tauga [present of food brought by a boy to a girl he is courting] but she mistrusts him. Admits a lover. Group in cahoots. Petting parties are group affairs—and yet they mistrust each other." In the book (1973:151–52) are described "three cousins who were popular with the youths of their own village and also with visitors from distant Fitiuta. . . . Namu was genuinely taken with a boy from Fitiuta whom she met in secret while a boy of her own village whom her parents favoured courted her openly. Occasional assignations with other boys of her own village relieved the monotony of life between visits from her preferred lover."

Subject 20 (pseudonym Tulipa): This subject, assigned the same pseudonym as subject 2 (who also has the same real name), does not appear in the book. The data in the binder are consistent with the tables but include in addition an interesting attitudinal comment: the subject, one of those in the petting parties just mentioned whose members mistrust each other, "admits she has had one lover and he came from Tutuila. Gossip has it that she was to marry the son of [a *matai*] . . . but this apparently is not so. Says she would like to marry, God and [her *matai*] willing. Is afraid to watch births—virginal in this among older girls."

Subject 21 (pseudonym Sala): This subject is one of the girls characterized by Mead as a "delinquent." The binder says that she "has a lover who sleeps there every night. . . . Charac-

terized by a [minister] as having 'only one skill—at the oldest
of professions.' . . . m [masturbates]. All her energies have
gone into sex." It would seem that some of this information
comes from an unmarried female informant whose age was
then twenty-two. The book notes (1973:181) that "Sala had
been sent to live in the pastor's house but had speedily got
involved in sex offenses and been expelled. . . . Her lovers
were many and casual, the fathers of illegitimate children,
men whose wives were temporarily absent, witless boys bent
on a frolic. It was a saying among the girls of the village that
Sala was apt at only one art, sex, and that she, who couldn't
even sew thatch or weave blinds, would never get a husband."
This lack of skill and even the note about "fathers of
illegitimate children" is supported by the data in the binder;
the source of the comment about her one skill has been
altered from that of a minister to the girls of the village,
perhaps to avoid attribution.

Subject 22 (pseudonym Tolu): The limited material in the
binder on this subject is on one point absolutely contrary to
what is in the book: "Says she doesn't want to marry for a
long while. Says she's too young." According to the book,
"Tolu, the eldest, was a little weary after three years of casual
adventures and professed herself willing to marry. She later
moved into the household of an important chief in order to
improve her chances. . . ."(1973:151). The binder does bear
out this change of residence; perhaps the comment by the
subject reflected a temporary viewpoint. The binder also says
that the subject was "very sensitive about love affairs."
Presumably this implies that she didn't want to talk about
them or hear talk about them.

Subject 23 (pseudonym Moana): This subject is the protago-
nist of one of Mead's most dramatic stories. According to the
binder, she

> doesn't want to marry, wants to go to school. Reported by sister
> to be musu to all lovers. Now has a nice one— "a handsome,
> faithful honorable boy" who [?]took proposal present and
> showed that his intentions were matrimony. He now sleeps there.

But subject will have nothing to do with him. Says she doesn't want to marry. Wants to go to school. She refuses to marry her cousin who seduced her also. She herself claims that the [affair with a male who was her *matai*] episode was true but seems [?]uninterested. [same male, pseudonym Mutu] claims it wasn't, but that she had been misbehaving and was turned over to his care by her mother, and that [same sister noted above] misinterpreted some circumstantial evidence. [?]Honors are easy on this point. She certainly has had sex experience. m [masturbates]. Is indolent, sensuous, [?]indifferent. Accepts [sister's] loving sisterly attentions as tributes to her superior good looks. [?]Intelligent.

One of the newsbulletins mentions the "intrigue with [*matai* noted above]. [He] was to perform the autopsy [on relative of the family of both the *matai* and subject 23] and remove the foetus and there was considerable controversy over this as he had been at enmity with the family for a month over his intrigue with [subject 23], granddaughter of [a *matai*] and at that time [*matai* noted above] adopted daughter."

The book closely follows the field data but with possible ambiguities ironed out and with considerable elaboration and interpretation of the role of subject 23's sister, who was in fact about seven years older than she (1973:155–56).

Perhaps the most dramatic story was that of Moana, the last of the group of girls who lived outside the pastor's households, a vain, sophisticated child, spoiled by years of trading upon her older half-sister's devotion. Her amours had begun at fifteen [her age in the census is given as fifteen, but since the tables indicate that her first menstruation was four years ago she is almost certainly older] and by the time a year and a half had passed, her parents, fearing that her conduct was becoming so indiscreet as to seriously mar her chances of making a good marriage, asked her uncle to adopt her and attempt to curb her waywardness. This uncle, who was a widower and a sophisticated rake, when he realised the extent of his niece's experience, availed himself also of her complacency. This incident, not common in Samoa, because of the great lack of privacy and isolation, would have passed undetected in this case, if Moana's older sister, Sila, had not been in love with the uncle also. This was the only example of prolonged and intense passion which I found in the three villages. . . . But Sila was devoted to Mutu, her stepfather's younger brother, to the point of frenzy. She had been his mistress and still lived in his household, but his dilettantism had veered away from her indecorous intensity. When she discovered that he had lived with her sister, her fury knew no bounds. Masked under a deep solicitude for the younger girl . . . she denounced Mutu the length of the three villages. . . . Village feeling ran high, but opinion was divided as to whether Mutu was guilty, Moana lying to cover some other peccadillo or Sila gossiping from spite. The incident was in direct violation of the brother and sister taboo for Mutu was young enough for Moana to speak of him as *tuagane* (brother). But when two months later, another older sister died during pregnancy, it was necessary to find some one stout-hearted enough to perform the necessary Cesarean post-mortem operation. After a violent family debate, expedience triumphed and Mutu, most skilled of native surgeons, was summoned to operate on the dead body of the sister of the girl he had violated. When he later on announced his intention of marrying a girl from another island, Sila again displayed the most uncontrolled grief and despair, although she herself was carrying on a love affair at the time.

Subject 24 (pseudonym Luina): This subject, as we have seen, is described in the binder as not masturbating, which is inconsistent with the book's table. She is described as "lazily promiscuous," apparently contradicting both tables, which indicate no heterosexual activity and have her living in a minister's household. She does not appear in the *CA* text.

Subject 25 (pseudonym Mina; the "Key to Namechanges" gives this name to another subject, but this seems incorrect): The binder mentions her as one of the few with "church membership" who did "not fall": "Takes very little interest in boys and accepts the fact that she will marry someday. Does not m." Again, the masturbation data is inconsistent with book's table. There is no mention of this subject in the book, perhaps because Mead had a particularly close connection with her and did not wish to risk her identification.

The binder contains sexual data on two adolescents (age eighteen) listed neither in the fieldnote table nor in Table I (Appendix V) of the book. Following the fieldnote table, these may be assigned the numbers 26 and 27 and provide this additional information:

Subject 26: "only [26] fell"; this refers to a heterosexual relationship while resident in the minister's household.

Subject 27: "Family boy given presents. Good deal less promiscuous than [?]theory."

Subjects 26 and 27 appear to add two clear cases of heterosexual experience to the fieldnote data, thus yielding 12/27 (44%) of the adolescents' having had such experience; if the sixteen-year-old premenarcheal case mentioned above (subject 28; *see* p. 26) is added, the total is 13/28 (46%), close to the percentage in *CA*'s Table I, 12/25 (48%).

A possible subject 29 appears in the binder and is assigned the pseudonym Tipolo in the "Key to Namechanges" but does not appear in the book; her age is only thirteen, and the binder says only that she has "lost interest boys to a certain extent."

Five additional girls are mentioned in the binder but not included in either table:

Subject 30 (pseudonym Lama): This subject, fourteen years old, is listed as an adolescent in Key Numbers, but no sexual data are provided in the field materials; perhaps this is because she had "gone back to [a different island]," according to the binder. In the text Lama is one of those "just approaching puberty," inconsistent with the listing in Key Numbers (1973:144).

Subject 31: About this fifteen-year-old, listed as an adolescent in Key Numbers but given no pseudonym, the binder indicates only that she has "not menstruated yet"; "no sex experience."

Subject 32: This thirteen-year-old is listed as an adolescent in Key Numbers but without a pseudonym. The binder says only that Mead "never succeeded in getting hold of her."

Subject 33 (pseudonym Vina): This subject is a fifteen-year-old listed as an adolescent in Key Numbers. The binder says only that she is "decidedly one of the younger of the adolescents." In the book she is made a year younger and is said to reside at an "extreme end of Siufaga" [actual village in which she lived], where relative isolation from other houses conditioned her social relationships (1973:65). Judging by the scheme of census notation, her residence would indeed have been at one end of the village. *CA* seems to have assimilated Vina into the category of those approaching puberty.

Subject 34: This subject is eighteen years old but is not listed as an adolescent in Key Numbers and has no pseudonym. The binder says only that some male subject is desired by subject 34.

In addition to the data on particular adolescent subjects, the binder also contains a variety of comments on matters related to sexuality. One of these comes from a twenty-two-year old with the pseudonym Sila who is the sister of subject 23. She tells of being "married when 15 against will. Husband used to beat her every night so she left him and came back to her real parents with her little boy whom she loved. 4 1/2 years later married fa'aSamoa [according to Samoan custom, i.e., not a church wedding] another man but he is making love to [subject 21]. . . . She did live in pastor's house but was banished." This same subject adds in a general vein that "if boy possesses a girl he'll run away." Though it is not absolutely clear from the binder, it appears that the same informant is the source of the following additional information: [?]children know who father of [subject's twenty-five-year-old female] child is." In the census Mead labels the subject a "prostitute," and she is the only subject so labeled there.

Mead says in the binder of this informant that "no amount of questioning reveals masturbation or homosexuality. If questioned as to pre-puberty sex activity expresses evident amazement & incredulity."

To two male informants, twenty-two and sixteen years old, respectively, Mead attributes the following remarks: "parents sleep here. Girls here. When parents sleep, girl runs away with a boy. They run to [?]this end of the village under a coconut tree. If they see another couple they hide. If a girl sleeps with two boys in one night, the first one is angry and fights with the second. Girls like to go walking in the moonlight, but boys don't. Boys are shy and don't wish to be seen. Always send a friend. It is a sa [forbidden] for a sister to act as soafafine [female go-between]. The advantage of a soafafine is that she can go to the girl in the day time. But a boy can only go at night."

From a male informant of twenty Mead records the following in the binder: "If there are many people around a girl never speaks to her sweetheart. She only talks with her eyes—or talks as signal." This informant seems to have provided some of the key data upon which Mead relies for her assessment of the force of religious chastisement for sexual violations. He says, "If Church members fall often, the time of probation for reinstatement is lengthened. . . . Sometimes the church members only scold and suspend the person from communion for 2 or 3 months. The best time for a girl to become Ekalesia [member of the congregation] is when she is grown up 18 or 19, and a boy when he is 20 or so. If younger brother desires very strongly to become Ekalesia they may—still they are too young."

The last of the informants on sex recorded in the binder is subject 15, an eighteen-year-old female. She says, "Samoan girls don't like to marry older men and usually their parents don't like for them to either. If the parents [?] it, the girl runs away to other aigas ['aigā] [family members]." She tells of someone's daughter who was unwilling to marry a minister who had tuberculosis: "She ran away to [so-and-so's place]. Soon her parents will have her again."

Mead has a brief account of what is apparently a scene she witnessed involving several young girls she classifies as "pre-ads" (preadolescents). It is not clear who is speaking, but the account in the binder runs like this: "Now then, get ready everybody at once. Shout them as fast as you can, together with [?]gestures and [?]illustration of [?]tickling pubic hair by carefully attaching one [?]bent hair to the knee. . . . [a preadolescent of unknown age] knew the most, with a [twelve-year-old preadolescent] running a close second. [A ten-year-old preadolescent] took a mischievous, noisey, less salacious delight in it all. . . . All got a little worked up. Pulled down shades and the [first preadolescent] danced a little more gaily than usual." This rather cryptic material is perhaps indicative of the kind of scene that might come to mind in characterizing attitudes to sexuality.

Judging by what Mead recorded in the fieldnotes, binder, letters, and news bulletins, she had a single informant on the details of sexuality. This informant was a man of about her age, spoke good English, and was a schoolteacher on the Island of Ta'ū but not in any of three villages in which she carried out the bulk of her work. Mead recorded in her fieldnotes the following material from this informant, whom she refers to here as "Amigo" (doubtless to maintain his anonymity in view of the intimate details regarding sexuality that he provides):

> If a girl elopes with a boy to his house the next morning her family will come to claim her. The father of the boy will ask the boy does he want to keep her—& I always say this, I just eloped with her for public information, she can go. Then she will cry and fall at his feet & beg him to keep her. So he can bear to hear her sorrow so he will run [?]away & tell his father to tell her to go home. And on the way home the family will beat her & maybe shave her head. If a boy goes after a girl and he is afraid of making her pregnant, he will try to [?]stop gradually because she will want him so much.

> If a girl refuses a boy it's a proof that she does not love him.

> When he has intercourse with a virgin, [?]uses [?]the [?]sheet [?]for blood & gives it to his family so all can know that she was a virgin.

> Thinks it takes 10 or 15 times of intercourse to get a woman pregnant. If a woman has had intercourse with several men, when she becomes pregnant the child is believed to be the child of the last intercourse. Only method of B.C. [birth control]

known is withdrawal. Often practiced. Then girl has no orgasm, is not [?]satisfied. Does not think this is good for girls but very much [?]afraid. At breaking of hymen girls cry & screem & often faint. 4 of his [?]numbers have fainted and if you are far away from a house you have to climb a low tree & get a coconut to pour on her face.

But she will like intercourse even the first time. If the veil is broken at 9 years can come back again at 12 & again at [?]—and she will like it. Has orgasm the first night. Girls orgasm usually after boys. If there is withdrawal woman not satisfied but man can usually come back very soon.

If a girl has intercourse once then boy goes away she will want it very much & wait for the first opportunity. [?]Only girls who have had intercourse a great deal want it more than men do. [?]Even true [?] [?]them out, refuse to let them withdraw.

[?]Many [?]married people have intercourse several times in one night. Known of 15 times in one night. Also couples go off in the bush in the daytime & and have intercourse and sleep. Usually intercourse takes only a minute or [?]so. Women when done then leaves or husbands excite them by handling. Boy have a definite technique of playing with breasts, with [?]limbs & labia, then navel, abdomen & clitoris and vagina [?] excite the girl. Never knew a girl, no matter how unwilling, who didn't get excited at this. Never knew of a frigid woman. Women have intercourse long after menopause, desire is very strong & like to entice young boys. And boys who can't get girls go to them. One old maid is [X] who is 38 & refused to marry. Only one in Samoa. Good many of the batchellors knew of a man who was too large and killed his wife 9 yrs ago in [village] and of an other man also huge who has been married [?] the [?] & killed all his wives. Some girls especially wantons like men who are big, other don't [?] making him sick to look at a big penis.

No other position than girl below [?]him. Though heard of the desirability of other positions—[?]can't work. Girl raises her knees & puts ankles over boys feet. Advice of mothers to girls on first intercourse is to lie very still & not kick and let the boy have his will. Boys who grow up without ever having broken in a virgin are very scarce. Don't know how to do it. In ordinary marriage 10 yards of white cloth must be procured & mothers look to see if daughters are virgins, & insist on cloth. If girl screems women come running. When hymen is broken [?]ilicitly, it's [?]chance believe girls word or boys [?] is to be [?] [thrown on ground] and later [?] away in the [?]brush. If a boy knows a girl is pregnant he will press her side [?] with his fist to produce an abortion because otherwise everyone would know he was a bad boy.

But some men like to get girls pregnant. Boys like virgins & girls like experience. Hymen is usually broken with fingers. Knows of a man who bit a girl's hymen off he was so excited. Girls, once broken, have no [?]long [?]tension in taking active part in ex[c]iting boy. Doubtful as to whether vaginal secretion was real semen or not. Girls masturbate by putting fingers inside & mimicking intercourse. Knows of cunilingus and felatio as preliminary to intercourse. No kissing or tongue kissing. Velovelo—sucking noise made by children [reduplicative for shooting a dart, or throwing a spear, etc.] is expressed on the grounds of the [?] sound of intercourse & [?]excitement surrounds adults sexually. All children have seen intercourse— and talked it over. Size of [?]men is considered by women in deciding on marriage. Oldest men can have intercourse, but only once a night—[?] [?]sharing. Doesn't know of impotense in any case nor of frigidity. Sexual intercourse is prolonged by play and talk together.

Though there is no date to mark this contribution, it is probable, judging both by the location of the informant and its place in the fieldnotes, that it was obtained late in February or early March 1926. Two years later Mead typed up the following note from the same informant:

[Informant] knew of one case of the perversion of a ten year old child by a 25 year old girl. Sometimes fathers moetotolo to daughters and brothers to sisters. If two couples live in the same house husband is always going to other woman. Yet he says men are more faithful than women. Pt of view is all. Withdrawal is practiced on Tutuila. Then girls is not satisfied. If a girl has had intercourse with several men the child is believed to be the child of the last pregnancy. Women slower than men. Women who have had much experience more amorous than men even.

Tire men out. Only lasts a very few minutes. Women who desire men excite them by handling. Boys proceed from breast, navel, abdomen, clitoris and vagina, using hands and lips. Women have intercourse long after menopause. Desire is very strong and try to entice boys. Desire is very strong. Boys who can't get girls go to them. Wantons like largeness. Knew of two bluebeards, one killed three wives. Advice of mothers to daughters is to lie still and not kick. Boys will try to abort girls because otherwise everyone would know he is a very bad boy. Boys like virgins and girls like experience. Hymen usually broken with fingers, occasionally bitten. Girls after virginity is lost have no hesitancy in taking the active part in exciting the boy. Asked whether vaginal secretion was semen or not. Girls masturbation mostly of mouth of womb. Cuninlingus and felatio both frequent as preliminary to intercourse. No kissing or tongue kissing. Vetovito, children's clucking. Size of man is considered by women in discussing marriage.

From the identical wording in places it is clear that portions of the note come from the handwritten material presented above. However, some of the material is not found in the handwritten note and is obviously important to Mead's understanding. Clearly, the typed version is in some instances simply a case of substituting standard English for the original colloquial expression or briefly summarizing. Perhaps material found in the typewritten account that does not appear at all in the original account is information that Mead remembered but had not transcribed. Examples of this are the "perversion of a ten year old child," the incestuous *moetotolo*, and the report of husbands' going to other women if they are joint residents. The rather disparate accounts of female masturbation in the two accounts remain puzzling.

Elsewhere in the fieldnotes there is another brief comment from the same informant that also occurs in a handwritten note and several years later in Mead's typewritten account. The handwritten comment reads: "[Subject] says: girls will all tell other girls how awful first night—how [?] she'll cry and kick and scream." The typewritten account says the following: "[Subject] says girls will always tell other girls how awful first night was, and make derogatory comments on lover's skill." Clearly, this "derogatory comments on lover's skill" is a rather substantial difference between the two.

In October 1925, about two months after Mead's arrival in American Samoa, she made a trip to a village on Tutuila. Here she spent ten days of which she says in a news bulletin that she "never spent a more peacefully happy and comfortable ten days in my life." Some impressions and data regarding sexuality were gleaned from this experience. A nineteen-year-old unmarried male who was the son of an important *matai* gave her the following information in English: "This informant makes a distinction between two kinds of people, those who are Christians and those who just believe in God and go to Church. Most of the Christians are older married people. Young people are not Christians except the girls who go to Atauloma [a girls' school run by the church]. When you get ready to get married, you repent and become a Christian. But the pastor will marry you even if you don't repent." This observation, obtained before Mead had even reached Manu'a, is exactly the one she maintains in the text.

A closely related viewpoint regarding the church and sexuality but more explicitly addressing itself to attitudes and practices was provided by an unmarried female teacher from Atauloma School for Girls. This interview occurred near the end of October at the school and is presented below in its entirety (typed fieldnotes):

> When a boy or girl come to a thinking age [probably a translation of *māfaufauga*] and wish to lead a good life, the pastor of the village must adopt them. The pastor's house is regarded as the only "safe house" in the village, the only place where "the line" is really drawn. These boys and girls live in the pastor's family and work for him as if they were his own children. They may or may not go home to eat. In any case the village provides the pastor with food so they are an asset rather than a financial burden. Boys to go to Malua [the theological college in Western Samoa] and girls who wish to go Atauloma must first have served a probationary period of varying length in the pastor's household. When these children return

home for vacations they must sleep in the pastor's household. Unchastity is punished by suspension from Church privileges, attendance at Communion and permission to stay for meetings from which other people are shooed out; girls are expelled from Atauloma and boys kept back two years from Malua from the time the sin is discovered. Formerly the commencement of the punishment dated from the commission of the sin, but some boys were so successful in covering their tracks that they would go through two years undiscovered and got to Malua when they ought never to have been there. If a pastor "falls" he loses his pastorate, and if his wife "falls" he loses his pastorate.

Q. Is there any attempt at confession, any feeling on the part of the young people that their sin has cut them off from God, and from religious privileges?

a. Oh no. They do their best to hide it. You see it is the ambition of every family to have one son go to Malua, and they make every attempt to cover up their tracks. But the girl's father, or some enemy usually tells in the end.

Q. Do they think God will punish them if they don't tell?

a. No. No taupou is ever allowed to be a member of the Church.

Q. But isn't that a contradiction? I understand that the taupou is supposed to be the virgin parexcellence, the one virgin in a village.

a. In theory, yes. But it's just that strict surveillance which makes her slip some night. And of course we have a few girls "go" every vacation one or two or three, either get married or go back to their old way of living. Our pastor in [village name] is so cynical that he simply refuses to admit anyone to communion who is not married.

Q. You say the girl, decides to live the good life, but surely those little eight and nine year olds that you have aren't come to years of discretion. I suppose you mean their father decided for them.

a. Oh no, you'd be surprised to see how young some of them begin talking about wanting to go to Atauloma. They hear the other girls talk about it you see, and they decide they'd like to go to.

Within days of Mead's arrival in Manu'a, a minister in one of the three villages "presented" her "with one of his 'good Christian girls' . . . what have decided to live the good life and are thereafter compelled to live in the pastor's household under exhausting scrutiny. . . to be my girl" (news bulletin VIII, p. 2). This young woman of twenty was said by Mead to speak no English, and her responses are indeed recorded in Samoan. About four days after Mead's arrival she recorded the following interview with this informant:

The Conduct of a Christian Girl   O le Amio o le Teine
Kerisiano

The Christian girl must want to adhere to Jesus, must have faith, conduct herself well, be of a quiet disposition and not dissolute, use good sense and serve God well and want to tell the story of Jesus, and serve him with a sincere heart, and adhere to the minister. She should not be bad hearted or jealous. She should not speak badly of others, but should speak well of them. She should obey the minister, listen to him, and show him respect. She should not be disobedient or unruly. Every Christian girl who desires close fellowship with Jesus and is sincere should sleep at the minister's house. The minister will not allow anyone who does not know how to behave to stay in his house. Should a girl marry a minister, her whole family will be pleased and there will be a big celebration. She cannot marry a young man who is related to the minister. However should he decide to go to Malua and she decide to go to Atauloma, they can get married.

About the same time as this interview, Mead writes in her news bulletin that "my good Christian girl, [name], will arrive to escort me to the afternoon service in [village name]" (VIII, p. 3). Another reference indicating attendance at church is noted in a news bulletin written less than a month after her arrival in Tutuila (V, p. 5), at a time when she clearly knew very little Samoan. She reports only that she went to church on Sunday and that "the sermon dealt largely with being a good flower giving forth a sweet odor," and the context for this obiter dictum is discussion of how Samoans take care to smell "sweet." A couple of months later she also attended a Sunday service, noting in a news bulletin (VIII, p. 3), "I was awakened at six by two maidens who insisted that it was time for Church, which really starts at 7:30. After Church, late breakfast and it is now 12:30, zero hour for heat. At 1:30 my 'good Christian Girl' [name], will arrive to escort me to the afternoon service in Faleasao, an abominably hot walk, and [the minister] warned me to start early because we would be so wet when we got there." This is the last reference to church attendance that she records, and she reports nothing either about the services or about other attendant events. Given that Samoans themselves attend church regularly and that Mead so early in her work had thoroughly discounted the influence of the church, it may well be that she continued to join her villagers in attendance without noting the event.

Whatever the facts may be regarding the church and sexual attitudes and practice, it seems clear that less than two months after arriving on Tutuila Mead was inclined to think of the restraint emanating from the church as none too stringent and to regard the girls as engaged in circumventing such restriction as there might be; she reports in a news bulletin of going out palolo fishing: "Boat loads of girls with their heads muffled in their lavalavas till they attained grotesque proportions. . . . The girls were muffled so the native clergy wouldn't recognize them, and the clergy prowled in paopaos (one man canoes) [small canoes] more intent on the non-appearing palolo." Clearly the "native clergy" already appear here as none too diligent. Though we have no direct information on how Mead reached this conclusion, it is difficult to believe that it was based solely on unaided observation. Perhaps it depended on prior belief or someone else's suggestion. She does not tell how the palolo expedition came about, but from the context it may have been in connection with her visit to the village of Leone on October 10. Here she met a "half caste" woman who spoke "English well" and her white mother and other members of the family.

This woman had lived in the United States for some time and was the wife of a former Navy man. Since this visit occurred in the daytime, it is possible that the evening expedition of October 10 was from Leone and that these people from Leone suggested the interpretation.

Indeed, four days earlier than the palolo expedition Mead wrote in a news bulletin (VI, p. 6) expressing her general impression of the weakness of "old tapus" (the Samoan word *tapu* means to be forbidden) and of contemporary Christianity:

> Also the fact that all the sanctions are social rather than religious seems to rob the culture of depth and intensity. The old tapus, never strong, have practically no force now, and a diluted Christianity, which consists mainly in the singing of impossible hymns and the praying of lengthy dull prayers, adds no glamour to the life. The whole thing is a life curiously lacking in depth, no dark malignant spirits prowl behind simple activities, graves are neglected in a year, rank is hedged about not with tapus, but with hairpulling, and the deepest crime is to make a mistake in a mans courtesy title. It is much easier to derive aesthetic pleasure from contemplating the ideas underlying their culture than from looking at the human embodiments of these ideas.

All of this was after a two-day trip, her "first real malaga" to the "far side of the island" with Dr. Ryan, his wife, their "cook boy," and a Samoan hospital worker as interpreter—part of an inspection tour under Navy auspices of village conditions. She had previously made more limited trips with the Lanes to villages that "skirted the road" but found these expeditions rather desultory. What she describes of this expedition is chiefly concerned with ceremonial greetings, presentation of kava, and the like. Having completed the expedition, she announces that she has "seen the principal social ceremonies of the Samoans, the Talolo, presentation of gifts, the sivasiva dance, the sword dance, and the kava ceremony." The gap between what she reports having seen and her rather categorical appraisal of tapus, sanctions, and the force of religious life certainly suggests strong presuppositions, especially when one considers how soon these pronouncements were made.

Later observations made in Ta'ū only reinforce these early impressions regarding religion and sexuality and provide some evidence of how the impression was sustained. Thus in a news bulletin (December 11, 1925) Mead writes of activities on a typical day and offers the following observations:

> and perhaps, just as we reach the store, the curfew-angelus will stop us, a wooden bell will clang mellowly through the village; The children must all scurry to cover, if we're near the store, it's the store steps, and sit tight until the bell sounds again. Prayer is over. Sometimes we are all back safely in my room when the bell sounds, and then the Lord's Prayer must be said in English, while flowers are all taken out of their hair and the siva song stopped in the middle. But once the bell sounds again, solemnity, never of a very reliable depth, is sloughed off, the flowers replaced in the girls hair, the siva song replaces the hymn and they begin to dance, by no means in a puritan fashion.

Here it is the lack of solemnity during religious performances and the perceived sexuality of the dance performed so soon after prayer that influence Mead's interpretation.

In her next-to-last news bulletin (XII [February 9, 1926]) Mead writes that two subjects "being married have now become church members," an event consistent with her account of the general separation of unmarried adolescents from full membership in the congregation. In the same news bulletin she reports a violation of church rules by a twenty-two-year-old preministerial student who has been ex-pelled and wants Mead to write "a long sanctimonious letter of repentance to the head of his preministerial school," using her typewriter. We are not informed of the nature of the violation.

Whatever Mead may ultimately have decided about the influence of Christian doctrine on Samoan life, she writes in a news bulletin (December 20, 1925) that "boarding school, in the pastor's house, is importing feminism into Samoa. The faife'au's girls don't want to marry and have children. They want to go to school all their lives."

There are a number of scattered remarks in the fieldnotes and elsewhere that bear on the question of sexual restraint and related matters. One of these notes, typed on March 29, 1928, concerns a number of rules and expectations regarding sexual behavior. The data come from a subject who is identified by name and as the wife of a named man; unfortunately, these names are not found in the census and cannot otherwise be identified. The fieldnotes contain the following information:

> She came from Tutuila. Only woman in love. Girl treats her father and mother in law with respect, joking and ugly words forbidden. They are ma [ashamed or embarrassed] of each other although no other taboos. It is bad to wish for the sex of a child for you always get the opposite. The woman should just sit. Women always want children at once. Some women are naturally jealous, others not. Very awkward, mataga [*mātagā*; also means "indecent"], for husband and wife to stay together and not sleep together.

As early as September 1925, on the visit to Vaitogi, Mead transcribed in Samoan the following interview regarding the brother-sister taboo with a young man who was the son of a *matai*:

> Once my sister is married I cannot go to her house anymore without good reason. The same applies to my sister. She will not be allowed to visit her brother and his wife at their house without good reason. The brother must never talk harshly or abusively to his sister. If my sister decides to do something she wants to do, she may do so. I have no right to speak against her wishes. I must always treat her with respect. If my sister is present in the house, I must seat myself properly. My legs must be positioned properly and no squatting. If my sister is visiting with her girlfriends, I cannot join them. It is forbidden for a brother to hold hands with his sister and to go out on a date with her.

At the end she appends a comment in English that this does not apply to young children and gives an example using the names of actual persons.

A very similar account of sibling relationships but with added detail on restrictions was also obtained in Samoan from an unmarried twenty-year-old Samoan female shortly after Mead's arrival in Manu'a and was typed on November 11, 1925. A month later typed notes containing further family restrictions were obtained from the wife of a *matai* and are recorded in English:

> First cousins as sa as brothers and sisters. If a girl runs away with an aiga the parents bring her back and scold her and tell her she must not do it again. If she persists, she is married to an old man for punishment and the boy is disinherited for a time. Goes to live with aigas on the other side of the house. But if the girl is pregnant they make them marry, but there is no feast, no exchange of property. The boy won't be pule [have authority] unless he works very hard for the matai. Will have to work much harder than other youths to reinstate himself.

There are references in the field materials to illegitimacy, adultery, abandonment, and abortion that also bear on the question of rules and adherence. On October 1, 1925, just over a month after her arrival in Tutuila, Mead attended a court session. One of the trials involved a violation of marriage law. She tells us that

> the judge is a Los Angelos politician, of conventional ideas but a fortunate lack of idealism in regard to the possibilities of enforcing his ideas in Samoa. There is also a Samoan judge, a reverend old chief of Fagata, but he seems to be just a figure head. The court record usually holds many entires of "No questions from Judge Luto." Every word said in court is interpreted by George Peters, A Samoan who hides his skill. [The case involved] a woman accused of marrying a husband in American Samoa while having a husband living in British Samoa. She was a great stout creature, spilling out of her clothes, with her lips pursed sullenly. When she spoke, it was as surprizing as if part of the hillside had suddenly begun to murmur in a gentle even tone. . . . She had come to American Samoa just to visit and left her husband and five of her seven children in Apia. Then her children write her their father living with another woman. Then her husband write her he satisfied with his new

woman, she can do what she likes. After a little while she marry
new husband to take care of her. The judge was magnificent.
He agreed to "forgive her bigamy" provided she would divorce
her husband and then legally remarry the man she was living
with. The woman agreed cursorily, without raising her eyes or
evincing any interest in the insane proceedings. "O lelei" [*ua
lelei*], Very good. . . . The whole affair is a glorious farce, with
the judge trying to be dignified and at the same time keep his
popularity with the people.

Clearly the language used indicates that the woman's testimony was given in English except for the exclamation after
the judge had rendered his decision. Mead's initial remarks
on the judge's recognition that he would not be able to
enforce his idealism on Samoans suggest that she regarded
the affair as at least not a very serious matter by Samoan
standards (news bulletin VI, p. 3).

Later in the month on her visit to Vaitogi Mead asked a
young unmarried woman if another young woman was
married; she replied "in the softest saddest voice in the world,"
and "whispered 'ua uma' [its' finished] and added that the
husband had gone to Upolu and never returned and that her
three children were dead" (news bulletin VII, p. 2). A couple
of weeks after her arrival on Ta'ū she mentions, in describing
the household of the Holts, in which she resided, that a
Samoan maid who served the family had a husband who
"deserted her and a baby who was dead" (news bulletin VIII,
p. 1 [November 14, 1925]).

In the typed fieldnotes (March 27, 1928) Mead lists five
couples as parents of "illegitimate" children in one of the
three villages; presumably these are not ambiguous cases
involving couples living together without church sanction,
since none of the females as shown by the census are living
with men with whom they are sexually linked. Four of the
five women listed are to be found in the census, and their
ages range from twenty to thirty. Three of the five males are
noted as being from elsewhere, and the two that are not are
not to be found in the census; one of them is listed as a

sixteen-year-old and the other as twenty-six. The other two
villages are not so treated in the fieldnotes. However, the
census indicates two illegitimate children in one of the other
villages. Either there were no such cases in the third village
or Mead had less detailed knowledge of this village. The sum
of known illegitimacy amounts to seven instances. There is
absolutely no indication of how illegitimacy was determined
in any instance or how Mead learned who the absent genitor
was. Perhaps she collected these data in developing her census,
since this is often where they are recorded. Though there is
no indication in the field materials how the census was
compiled, it is possible, judging by its form, that the essential
facts of family membership were provided by a church census.

In a news bulletin written in December 1925, shortly after
her arrival in Ta'ū, Mead describes a tense gathering that also
bears on the question of sexual mores. The group involved
consisted of a European, a *matai* from one of the three
villages, and several others. The European had a Samoan wife,
but Mead notes that the *matai* was the father of one of the
European's children. "They sat and glared at each other, [the
matai] with a gay insolence which he wears well despite his
two hundred and fifty pounds; [the European] irritable and
blond, telling [the *matai*] that no one in [a European country]
had ever heard of Samoa."

Just above the "illegitimacy" data, Mead writes of an
"elopement" [*āvaga*] from the same village. It names the
subject, gives her age as twenty-five, and says that she "ran
away to [village name] with [the son of the village] chief.
Marriage has passed as family refused to give property, girl
was punished. Now lives with her father, [name]." The census
also notes this as a "runaway marriage" but has the woman's
age as twenty-nine. In the same village mentioned as having
two illegitimate children, an additional "runaway marriage" is
noted between a twenty-eight-year-old male and a female from
the same village whose age is not given.

However casual Mead may have thought the Samoans were

about sexual bonds, the formal interview data on infidelity appear inconsistent with this impression. In an interview with the wife of the same *matai* who gave her the account of cousin and sibling relationships provided earlier, Mead obtained the following (typed fieldnotes, November 28, 1925):

> Murder was very rare in Samoa, only occurring when two people got into a fight and one hit the other with something too heavy. Then he would not run away, he would just come home and say I killed him. Then maybe the other family, the family of the boy who was killed would try to kill him.
>
> But in the case of adultery, the man will flee to the bush and the husband may kill him and there will be no blood revenge because he had a right to kill him. Sometimes he will kill his wife too. If he wants to take his wife back, he may but his family will not like it and they will not respect her as the chief's wife anymore. They will feed her because they have to, but they will not respect her, so usually she will go and live with her own family. If the adulterer escapes, then the family of the injured man will try to kill some member of the adulter's family. In that case the adulter's family will IFO [make a formal apology].

On the same page Mead records that a *matai* from Vaitogi told her that "adultery was punished with slavery or tue le paepae" [*tu'i le paepae* = destroy the raised stone platform on which a house is built; elsewhere on the page it is spelled tuipaepae]; from the same informant Mead notes that the punishment known as "tue le paepae" is one in which "all the possessions of a man were confiscated and his house raised to the ground, his pigs killed. His permanent property, fine mats and siapo [bark cloth], became the property of the village and were kept for ifoing to another village." It is of course notable and relevant to our understanding that all of this is narrated in the past tense; however, this last account is relevant to at least the rather recent past, since the narrator recalls such an instance during his lifetime: "[informant] remembers when a man named [name] who lived in [village in Tutuila], spread a rumour that a malaga [here, group making a trip] of the chiefs of his district has all been put into gaol in Upolo. When the chiefs came back they went and tue le paepae."

Whatever Mead may have been told, it seems that she at least discounted the severity of the punishment meted out for adultery. Writing a summary for herself on various subjects (January 4, 1927) she says that "adultery was punished with slavery, tuipapepae or banishment, or drownding if the lady was chief's wife. This is mainly talk. Slavery meant doing a large chore for the village, not real slavery. Road making was a favorite form of punishment for breaking a tulafono, a village law." She continues: "Murder and adultery were private affairs unless they affected village feuds. Incest a village concern." Unfortunately, the summary makes no reference to the sources for these conclusions.

In a similar summary on property she writes, "More serious offenses such as adultery with the chief's wife, outraging the taupo, involving the village in an actual war with another village, treachery in time of war, spreading scandal about one's own village, were punishments by a wholesale destruction of property known as tui-paepae, which means raising a house to the ground. . . . " The chronologically last obtained reference on adultery was recorded by Mead during her trip to Ofu in early March 1926. Here she was told by a *matai* that "incest punished with banishment, or if far enough away and girl pregnant with marriage" (typed notes, March 30, 1929).

In typed fieldnotes (March 28, 1928) Mead provides a lengthy commentary on aspects of sexuality connected with childbirth; some of this material was provided by an "old midwife" and the rest by a "nurse," these interviews being held in a village other than the three where Mead generally worked but on Ta'ū probably late in February or early in March 1926 (news bulletin XIII, p. 3, [March 7, 1926]). In this news bulletin Mead says, "But [name] (the nurse's notion of interpreting is to repeat the same thing to me in Samoan) and the old midwife stayed behind to tell me some stories she wouldn't tell [name] because she came from another village. So I gave up attempting interpreters and worked on everything from religion to medicines without them." However this may be, the fieldnotes are largely in English for both subjects. The part about abortion is interspersed with other commentary from the old midwife much of which is relevant to our interests:

> Tell pregnancy by the breasts, brown and swollen. Morning sickness begins at end of first month. Some women have none, some a week, some a month. 1 month's menstruation missed counted as pregnant. Never saw menstruation during pregnancy. Up to the second months a girl can procure an abortion by drinking kava, or by chewing kava and swallowing it. kava is sa to pregnant girls. Also lomilomi [massage] will work up to the second month. No punishment of any sort ana mua [olden days]. Advice to the pregnant: Don't eat walking, don't eat secretly. Don't eat hot food, don't drink a coconut until someone else has drunk from it, don't cut meat near mouth. Can only eat o'o [germinating coconut] if it is swollen to whole inside of shell, not otherwise. Sa to weave for a long time. Sa to go anywhere toatasi [singly]. Intercourse always is likely to produce abortion. Should be no intercourse until a year after birth. (this is juts midwife's twaddle. never observed.) One method for abortion. Some women nurse during beginning of pregnancy and don't know they are pregnant because some women don't menstruate between pregnancies. Conception sometimes occurs just before menstruation and first menstruation can then follow. Intercourse during menstruation is not sa. It is impossible to conceive during the period. Penalties for breaking taboos: for cutting with knife, hair lip. eat while walking, she has a runaway child, drink a full coconut, child will gulp and not swallow milk, eat's loose o'o [germinating coconut] miscarriage, eats alone, birth marks and too many fingers or too many toes, hot food, child is blistered. Pregnant woman is allowed to look at anything, a delivery, a post mortem caesarian. Hard labor and children dead due to angry aiga ghosts. The foetus was thrown outside the fence, nowadays wrapped in siapo and buried. It is born in 9 or 10 months and comes back and cries if it were not properly buried. If this were so there was nothing to do, and yet formerly they were afraid to handle the foetus and so threw it away. For

a miscarriage, vai samasama [*vai* = water, *samasama* = yellow; perhaps turmeric in water] ointment, not made by midwife, rubbed over body. A well formed miscarriage was wrapped in lau u'a [mulberry leaf] and then in siapo. [Nurse] says seven month babies will live but 8 month babies won't. Nothing to do for too early births? Use vai mumu [red water]. Valu ao'a [eight banyan] leaves, pestle it. mix with water and give to the babies to drink, then use ointment to spread over the body of the baby. This ointment is made of an ointment for which are either chewed or pounded 4 leaves of toga [?] and four leaves of avavaiaitu [a shrub, *Piper insectifugum*].

Following this account there is a shorter paragraph apparently also taken from the midwife; it is labeled "Tale of [name's] household god":

A girl was pregnant and miscarried. She called her brother and he gave her his head circlet of white siapo and she wrapped the foetus in it and threw it i uta [inland]. The brother and sister died and became stones. But the chief, father of the child, found the siapo, opened it and the child moved and cried and breathed. It was fed and tended by a bird called miti [cuckoo shrike or triller] and a bird called tuli [name given to several birds] and called the manu ali'i [chiefly bird].

In further typed fieldnotes (March 22, 1927) the same midwife comments on menstruation:

A girl will die if she doesn't menstruate. A girl may not marry till she menstruates. A girl can't make 'ava [kava], help in the ceremony or drink it until after she has menstruated. No feast or presents mark the beginning of menstruation. Some girls and women have no sense, "le ai se maufaufau" [*māfaufau*] and hide their condition and do not observe the menstrual taboos. Some girls menstruate once some twice a month. A girl can bathe, dance and go i uta [inland, to the "plantation"]. Should stay in a different house from her brother. No special house ever known. Late menstruation makes a girl pale and have swelling abdomen. No St. Vitus dance known. Very cross and irritable as are menstruation girls. Cry easily, anger easily, don't want to eat, finicky about food. Same at menopause.

There are a few additional scattered notes concerning

menstruation. One of these is contained in handwritten fieldnotes without a date and is in Samoan. The informants appear to be five girls, all from a single one of the three villages; the oldest is twenty and the next oldest is fifteen and both are among the adolescents included in Mead's tables. The other three consist of twins aged ten and a half and a nine-year-old. The information concerns instruction on first menstruation:

> The girl is instructed not to get cold or bathe in cold water. She should boil some water and then mix it with cold water until lukewarm before she bathes. She is also told not to bathe in sea water. She may help her mother make the umu [oven] or go to the plantation to cut down bananas or weed the taro patch. She may weave blinds, food platters and baskets or make siapo. She may also fetch water to drink or pick up the trash. Anything sa? Some girls may go dancing, some are not allowed. They cannot play any sports up to 3rd day. Parents will not allow them.

The only additional note on menstruation is contained in typed fieldnotes (March 28, 1929), and the informant appears to be an elderly woman who was the mother-in-law of an important chief. It is recorded in mixed Samoan and English: "Sa to menstruating women to valu o'a [scrape coconut husk]. Sa to taele [*tā'ele* = bathe] in the sea if valu o'a that day. And intercourse night before is sa. Some women are very desirous at menstruation, others musu lava [very reluctant]."

There are two references in the field materials that bear directly on the question of the *tāupou* and virginity. The first of these comes from the wife of a chief (typed fieldnotes, December 15, 1925) and is almost entirely in English:

> There are two big marriages, from the standpoint of a single village, the marriage of the taupou and the marriage of the "Manaia." The Manaia is the chief's son or other relative in his household who is nominally chosen to succeed his father. He is the one whom the chief says the others must "respect." Sometimes there is a ceremony when he is chosen, sometimes no. . . .

In proposals of marriage between the manaia and a taupou the manaia first sends a tulafale [talking chief]. He will bring a present of some food and talk to the girl's father. Then he goes back and the girl's father talks to the girl and asks her opinion. If there are two contestants the village talks it over and decides which alliance it prefers. The father make [perhaps "may"] tell the village that the girl is unwilling to marry someone, but they may decide to marry her to him just the same. If a chief is stingy (manumanu) [covetous or envious] he may decide to keep his taupou a while and offer a younger daughter in marriage. The proposing village must decide whether they will accept her or not. The manaia himself never appears until his proposals have been informally accepted. Then he and his tulafales and tulafales sons, and in fact practically all the men of the village come over the villages and bring maybe ten pigs according to their wealth. The two sides have a formal meeting in the house of the girl's father, where the tulafales of both sides made speeches. The boy's tulafales praise the girl and her village and vice versa. Then the visiting party goes home, with the exception of two or three tulafales and perhaps also tulafales sons who are left by the suitor to watch over his bride to be. Then the taupou and her tulafales eat up the pigs having a grand feast. The men of the boys party who are left behind have to work for the father of the taupou. He keeps two or three of them and distributes the others in the houses of other chiefs. They eat and sleep in the houses of these chiefs and every Sunday they get a new siapo as a gift. The time that the marriage is to take place is agreed on at this preliminary meeting—the nearer the villages, the shorter the space in between. If the girl doesn't behave the tulafales first remonstrate with her father. If he does nothing, then they go home and the marriage is off. Behavior of an engaged girl consists in staying very quietly in doors, in not going about with other girls and in never even speaking alone to another boy. This is the time when she elopes if she wishes to marry some boy in the village. If she has had a real or would be lover in the village, he is likely to throw disrepute upon her virginity if he is chagrined. Such a boy is called a pua'a, pig. The manaia's whole village comes for the wedding, coming about two days before. The taupo's village has decided on the billeting of the guests before they arrive—all the matais are put into one house, all the women into another. Then every night there is much festivity. The boys go to call on the visiting girls and the girls on the visiting boys. For the wedding the two parties sit opposite each other in the malae [open space or "village green"]. . . .

There is no fixed rule that oldest must marry first. if the taupou is a good girl and attracts lots of people to her father's house, then he may give one of younger sisters or cousins in marriage. If a younger sister wishes to marry on her own hook father may tell her to wait, unless he thinks she is too wild and likely to run off. Then he will rather let her get married. If a boy ran off with the girl to whom a member of his family was engaged he would be disowned and disgraced by his family.

Virgins formerly left their hair long on top and shaved the sides. This was permitted to grow long on marriage. If a girl eloped or became pregnant her head was shaved that all might know her disgrace. Virgins haircut, fa'amalumalu [literally, "to be sheltered"]. . . .

In the marriage of the taupou the tokens of virginity are taken by the boy's tulafale. In the marriage of an ordinary girl, the ceremony takes place in the house, only the family and the boy's friends are present and some older man chosen by the boy, performs the ceremony. No relative of boy is preferred.

From the same informant (typed notes, November 28, 1929) comes the following on "runaway marriages":

If the taupou wishes to marry she must consult the tulafale. If they will not let her, or if her father objects, then sometimes she runs away. The friends of the groom sing "Le ulo lea ua tini tinio" [*ulo* = pot; *tini* = chant; *tinio* = hurry], to advise her father of the fact. Then her family go and get her and bring her back and shave her head. If she tries to run away again they tie her up to a post and beat her. The members of the boy's family beat him. if the marriage is to be recognized, the boys family must come and get the girl, but because her head is shaved everyone will know that she ran away.

As for the behavior of the daughter of a chief, this same informant adds: "People do not have to respect her and obey her as they do a taupou. And when she goes abroad she does not have to have a chaperon with her. She may run around quite freely with the other girls, and they will only respect according as she behaves with dignity or runs about like a child."

Mead's other informant on the *tāupou* and virginity appears to be a high chief living in one of the three villages (typed notes, April 14, 1927, or p. 2, 2nd box, handwritten notes). The relevant material begins with the word "Fa'amaiseao" [*fa'amāsei'au* = deflower]; and continues:

> The defloration ceremony. Occurs after the property exchange, in the evening with the house brilliantly lit. The girl is frightened and ashamed. If she is not a virgin she should tell the talking chief so that their ceremony will be omitted. If she proves not to be a virgin all the old women in her family will beat her and beat her and her husband will despise her. But if she is a virgin the talk will go all over Samoa. The Tulafale of the husband wraps his first and second fingers with white tapa and breaks the hymen. He gives a shout if she proves to be a virgin and all the people beat pates [?pots] and break coconut shell and sticks. Make as much noise as possible. Then he walks around and lets each tulafale smell his fingers. Formerly intercourse followed at once in the presence of all the spectators. Then a big feast followed. If the girl was a virgin, her mother in law and all the older women of her husband's household crowded about her and wept over her and thanked her for the honor she had brought to their house. Ten yards of white tapa was used to stem the blood and this bloody banner was then suspended outside the house for all to gaze upon and be happy. If a boy elopes with a taupo he may not live with her if he thinks her family will consent to the marriage, for then he can have the defloration ceremony. But if he thinks her family will object or the girl seems only half won then he will live with her to further bind her to him. if the girl is eloping of her own free [?will] the tulafale of her lover will throw a stone into the house at night and she will slip out and run away with her lover.

There are a number of accounts regarding relations between boys and girls. One of these is entirely in Samoan as transcribed by Mead and handwritten; unfortunately, there is no date or reference for the informant:

> Differences in the conduct of boys and girls.   A boy is allowed
> to go out and play or go visit other families. He may play by
> himself or if he sees other children then he may join them and
> play together with them. Then he may return home. A girl may
> also go play with other children or play with her father and
> mother. She may play by herself where her mother can find
> her easily. Before she goes out to play she is brought into the
> house and cautioned or advised to behave and not be unruly.
> She is told to listen well to her parents. She cannot stay home
> alone. She can go with her parents.   The 13 year old girl
> behaves differently. She cannot go where boys are. Its harder
> for girls because parent's discipline harder. She cannot play
> with boys or go anywhere by herself. The parents can discipline
> and teach her so that she is well-behaved. She may not attend
> any sports for boys. It is forbidden to play ta ti'a [*tāgāti'a* =
> darts], nor can she tilitili [fish with a casting net]. She cannot
> act like a tomboy or go with boys. Some girls are allowed and
> some not to go with boys to the plantation. Girls can walk with
> boys on the road as long as they are going in different directions.

In typed fieldnotes (March 29, 1928) Mead generalizes for
herself, noting that "youthful conversation in groups trades
on sex, accusation of amorousness and moetotolos, also
accusations of greediness, delight in giving false names and
use of hyperbole." Such a commonplace teasing sort of
repartee is recorded in Mead's news bulletin of January 23,
1926. Present were five young males, two twenty-two years old,
one eighteen, one fifteen, and one of unknown age not
included in the census; one young female of eighteen was
present and of course Mead herself. One female, also not in
the census, is referred to in the conversation. Though the
bulletin was written for its English-speaking readers, it seems
that the conversation was chiefly in English with a few Samoan
phrases; it is difficult to imagine that a word like "dude" in
the conversation is a translation of Samoan, but Samoan
phrases do appear occasionally.

Says [name], the only girl present: "I'm going back to Apia on the next boat". "Why?" "She wants to see her sweetheart". "He's a liar, I have no sweetheart". "She's a liar, she has many". "How many?" Makelita [Samoan for Margaret], ask [male name of unknown age] how many sweethearts she has?" "How many, [male of unknown age]?" "Ten". "Oh, he is a liar". "Makelita, hold the court again to decide if [male of twenty-two] and [female present] are relatives." From [male of twenty-two], "Aua, (don't)." "Well, who will be witnesses?" "[name of male of eighteen]". From [male of eighteen] hastily, "I know nothing about it." "Well then, how are you related, [female present]." [female present], dubiously, "Our fathers are brothers". General mirth. Diversion. "[second male of twenty-two] is a great dude, he loves to wear flowers behind his ear". From [second male of twenty-two] "My eye hurts, I'm wearing these flowers to shield it from the light". "Maklita, who are you wearing that rose in your hair for?" "For all of you". "Not for [female present], a girl doesn't wear flowers for a girl." This from all. [female present] yawns. It is eleven o'clock. "I'm going home". "Who will escort you?" "[male of fifteen]." General hilarity. "Tele tautala laititi [very impudent, specifically impudence of the young acting "above their station"] [male of fifteen]. ([male of fifteen] is always running after older girls.) "Who's your girl [male of fifteen]." From [another male of fifteen], "[female of unknown age not present]". [male] who is fifteen and six feet giggles in agony. "Ask [female not present] tomorrow Makelita." From [male of fifteen] in agony not one whit assumed, "O Makelita, DONT." From [female of eighteen], "I'm sleepy. I'm going home and I'm going alone." "Tofa [goodbye], [female of eighteen]. Soi Fua [*soifua* = goodbye, literally "live"], Makelita." [female of eighteen] reaches the door, and turns: "[male of eighteen], sau i [come on]!" And [male of eighteen] leaps to his feet and follows her.

As Mead says in the binder, "A perpetual joke is whether a boy or girl are lovers or relations."

Notes, Chapter 3, Adolescent Sexuality: "Just the Facts"

1. A question mark in brackets followed by a space indicates an undeciphered word; a question mark in brackets before a word or number indicates uncertainty about the word or number.

4

Adolescent Sexuality: "Degrees of Freedom"

One of Freeman's strongest criticisms of Mead concerns her depiction of Samoan adolescents, with the exception of the *tāupou*, as engaging in considerable premarital sex under little if any adult constraint. This impression of Mead's view is supported by a number of quotations from her works and the comments of various of her readers. Thus chapter 16 ("Sexual Mores and Behavior") of Freeman's book begins by suggesting that the popular appeal of *CA* was largely due to its "alluring portrayal of Samoa as a paradise of adolescent free love" (1983a:226). In support of this view Freeman notes that Mead speaks of premarital lovemaking as the Samoans' "pastime par excellence" (Mead 1929:269); he adds that she claims lovemaking "was free" and, again quoting her (1973:195), that girls deferred marriage "through as many years of casual love-making as possible." He points out that two eminent anthropologists concluded from Mead's work that "free love" was the prevailing Samoan adolescent pattern: Honigmann characterized Samoan culture as embracing "institutionalized premarital sexuality" (1963:273), and Robert Lowie, reviewing *CA*, said that "Miss Mead's graphic picture of Polynesian free love is convincing. It falls into line with the reports of early travellers" (Lowie 1929:532). The use of "free love" to describe the Samoan practice is approximated by Mead herself in a 1937 publication in which she speaks of the rivalrous situation between young men "in the free love-making which precedes marriage" (1937:310).

Confining ourselves to *CA*, there are certainly other lines that contribute to an impression of "free love" or "free experimentation" among Samoan adolescents. For example, Mead lists among the factors limiting sexual hang-ups "the freedom to experiment" (1973:158). Indeed, "opportunity to experiment freely" leads the list of factors that limit conflicts arising from sexual experience (160). Very early in *CA* Mead says of the Samoan adolescent girl over fourteen that "all of her interest is expended on clandestine sex adventures . . . "(33). It may well be, however, that our impression of "free love" rests more on Mead's evocative descriptions than on explicit generalizations. One reads of a moonlit scene in which there are "shouts of triumph or disappointment, teasing words or smothered cries of outraged modesty. Or a group of youths may dance for the pleasure of some visiting maiden. . . . a circle from which every now and then a few will detach themselves and wander away among the trees. . . . the mellow thunder of the reef and the whisper of lovers, as the village rests until dawn" (19). Without belaboring the point, there are clearly grounds for Freeman's characterization of Mead's portrayal of female adolescent sex and for the impressions of others.

These generalizations and descriptions cannot, however, reflect Mead's understanding of the situation, for she explicitly notes three limitations on the "free" sexuality of female Samoan adolescents. The first of these is related to rank. Mead's somewhat equivocal statement of this limitation follows a lengthy discussion of "formal sex relations": "in such manner are conducted the love affairs of the average young people of the same village, and of the plebeian young people of neighboring villages" (1973:97–98). The equivocation arises from the lack of specification of the criteria for distinguishing the "average" and "plebeian" from the elite. The sentences that follow might be taken to mean that only the *tāupou* was meant to be excluded from such free sexuality: "From this free and easy experimentation, the taupo is excepted" (1973:98). Then, after some discussion of the virginity testing of a *tāupou*, Mead continues: "Although this virginity-testing ceremony was theoretically observed at weddings of people of all ranks, it was simply ignored if the boy knew that it was an idle form, and 'a wise girl who is not a virgin will tell the talking chief of her husband, so that she be not shamed before all the people' " (98). Shortly thereafter, however, Mead makes it clear that the restriction applies to others as well as the *tāupou* (99–100):

> Just as the clandestine and casual "love under the palm trees" is the pattern irregularity for those of humble birth, so the elopement has its archetype in the love affairs of the *taupo,* and other chief's daughters. These girls of noble birth are carefully guarded; not for them are secret trysts at night or stolen meetings in the day time. Where parents of lower rank complacently ignore their daughters' experiments, the high chief guards his daughter's virginity as he guards the honour of his name, his precedence in the kava ceremony or any other prerogative of his high degree. Some old woman of the household is told off to be the girl's constant companion and duenna.

Doubtless it has been disappointing for some to have learned that the "trysts under the coconut trees" were not for all, but perhaps many of us were relieved to think that noble birth and chiefs would not have restricted many. Experts, however, would have realized that in the rather bilateral system of Samoan descent (which can, with varying degrees of success and in various contexts, be traced through ascendants of either sex, e.g., through father or mother) few are unable by their own devices or with help to claim the "noble birth" that entitles one to a connection with some coveted title and, perhaps more important, that most Samoan men attain a title of some kind by middle age. Often, then, Samoan adolescents will have fathers who have titles, and most will live in households under the authority of a titled person. The hierarchy of titled persons throughout Samoa is complex, and from hints in *CA* and from more detailed description in *Social Organization of Manu'a* (1969) some of the relevant Manu'an hierarchy can be made out. However, the data on adolescents are far too thin to determine what role if any rank may have played in deterring adolescent female sexual adventures. What data there are of this kind are rendered inconsequential by the strong effect of the other two restrictive factors—age and/or time since first menstruation and residence in the pastor's house.

If we roughly divide titles into high and low on the basis of the indications of Mead (1969) and Holmes (1957), twenty-one of Mead's adolescent girls were from the households of low rank and two from those of high rank; one additional girl shifted from the household of a high to a low *matai*. One was the daughter of a minister. However, the two from high-ranking households were respectively only two months and six months past menarche, and therefore it would be absurd to attribute their lack of sexual experience to their household's rank. There were five additional adolescents in three high-ranking households that Mead did not study; two of these girls were reported to be not "fullblooded" Samoans and may have been excluded for this reason. Clearly, Mead's conclusion about the closer scrutiny provided by those of high rank is not based on empirical evidence of such scrutiny.

The only data in the field materials that explicitly refer to this question of rank and permissiveness are contained in an interview in Leone with a woman named Helen Ripley Wilson. Mead lists her as an "informer" and notes that she is a "halfcaste daughter of an Upolu woman, educated in Honolulu; in close contact with the chiefs of the island; has accurate knowledge and pride in Samoan people and their customs." This interview took place on October 10, 1925, less than six weeks after Mead's arrival at Tutuila. It included the following description of Samoan practice regarding girls and sexual permissiveness:

> Girls, even of common families, are never sent from village to village singly, without an older woman if possible. It was not considered right to send a girl when there were plenty of men around the place. Girls of no rank were allowed to go from house to house to house alone. A women of high standing does not go from house to house, that it may not be said that she is a gossip and goes from house to house spreading scandal. She may only go to the houses of women of the same rank, or to the wives of talking chief's if she is the wife of a chief. For the wife of a high chief it is even harder to go among the people.

Wilson's statement that "girls, even of common families," are chaperoned but that "girls of no rank were allowed to go from house to house" might well be the basis for Mead's contentions regarding rank and chastity. The informant's stated restrictions on girls of common families and, by implication, those above them has been narrowed by Mead to daughters of "noble birth." At the same time she has, of course, broadened the range of permissiveness by implying that it applies to all those of less than "noble birth." Any observer of Samoa is likely to have heard claims like this one and it may well be that higher status is accompanied by greater restrictions. The difficulty, however, is that "no rank," "common families," and "noble birth" have no clear boundaries, nor could they in a society in which with ingenuity and interest anyone can stake out claims of rank (though making such claims stick may well be a lifetime task).

The second limitation of sex is age, which is explicitly noted by Mead: "perhaps a year, two or even three years would pass before a girl's shyness would relax, or her figure appeal to the roving eye of some older boy" (1973:146). Her tables certainly support such an age limitation (Table II; 286–87).

Table 2

Heterosexual Experience by Time Elapsed since First Menstruation

	Fieldnote Table		CA Table 1	
Time	+	-	+	-
2 mos.	0	4	1[a]	3
3 mos.	0	2	0	2
6 mos.	0	1	0	1
1 yr.	1	0	2	0
1.5 yr.	0	1	0	1
2 yrs.	1	3	1	3
3 yrs.	6	1	6	1
4 yrs.	2	1	2	1
5 yrs.	0	1	0	1
Total	10	14	12	13

[a] This discrepancy is probably due to counting *Subject 4*, Leta, who was raped at eight, as having had sexual experience in the latter table but not in the former.

Excluding the single case of alleged rape, no heterosexual experience is indicated for the first year after the onset of menstruation. For one year after menstruation the fieldnote table has one case and that subject is positive for heterosexual experience; Mead's table 1 has two cases and both are positive. The second positive case (subject 8) is discussed in the binder, which, as we have seen, equivocally supports the positive designation. According to the census, both these adolescents are seventeen, which is somewhat older than might be expected if they first menstruated about a year earlier. For the first two years since menstruation the fieldnote table shows only two cases of thirteen to be positive for heterosexual experience and *CA*'s Table I three of fourteen (excluding the rape case).

Most of the girls (eight of eleven) three years past menarche had had heterosexual experience. Clearly it is these late adolescents, ranging in age from fifteen to twenty with a median age of eighteen, who constitute the bulk of those said to have had heterosexual experience. In fact, there are only two cases of heterosexual experience for girls under seventeen.

The third factor limiting sex, according to Mead, is residence in the pastor's household. She says, "A glance at the table in the Appendix will show that among the girls a couple years past puberty, there is a definite inverse correlation between residence at home and chastity, with only one exception, Ela, who had been forgiven and taken back into the household of a pastor where workers were short" (1973:147). Indeed, the relationship is quite strong (Table 3).

Table 3

Heterosexual Experience by Residence in Pastor's Household for Those Two or More Years Past First Menstruation

Residence	Fieldnote Table		CA Table I	
	+	-	+	-
Pastor's Household	1	6	1	5
Not in Pastor's Household	8	0	8	1
Total	9	6	9	6

chi square = 11.43; sig. at .001; phi = .87   chi square = 7.82; sig. at .05; phi = -.72

These figures alone do not tell us whether or to what degree it is the supervision or the girls' preferences, attitudes, and beliefs that results in the abstinence; perhaps family preferences are also relevant.

There is, however, some reason for doubt about the precision of the figures relating residence in the pastor's household to time since first menstruation (Table 4).

The oddity is, of course, that of the newest adolescents (two months), three of four reside in a pastor's house; the number

Table 4

Residence in Pastor's House by Time since First Menstruation		
	Residence	
Time	+	-
2 mos.	3	1
3-18 mos.	0	6
2 yrs.	4	0
3-4 yrs.	0	10
5 yrs.	1	0
Total	8	17

Note: The fieldnote table shows one less resident in the two-year category.

then drops to none for the adolescents in the next category, rises to four of four for those two years into adolescence; and drops again to none for the next category. There is also some doubt about the reliability of the time since first menstruation since these figures indicate that about one-sixth (four out of twenty-four in the fieldnote table, four out of twenty-five in *CA*'s Table I) of the adolescents first menstruated two months ago, which is obviously unlikely.

Whatever our doubts about the reliability of these tabulations, Mead's understanding of the situation must have been a "freedom" limited by rank, sexual maturity, and residence with a pastor. These limitations are meant to account for the fact that *CA*'s Table I, as Freeman has noted (1983:238), shows only twelve of twenty-five (48%) as having had heterosexual experience; since one of these was a childhood rape case, the relevant figure is really eleven of twenty-five (44%). The fieldnote table and data in the binder yield the closely comparable figures of thirteen of twenty-eight (46%).

But how reliable is the evidence on actual sexual experience? Here we are speaking not of general impressions but rather of specific facts about individuals. There is virtually nothing in *CA* about how Mead gained such information. From the binder and other field materials scattered statements relevant to this question can be assembled. If one examines the thirteen cases of alleged heterosexual activity just noted with an eye to credibility, what is most striking is the sketchiness of references regarding sources and the virtual absence—even when a source is indicated—of information on how a response was elicited. Six of the references have no source whatsoever; three indicate the subject herself; three might well be termed gossip, the source indicated as "other girls," "younger girls," or "theory," and one additional "gossip" is mentioned as a source additional to the subject herself; for two subjects specific sources other than the subject herself are noted (an unmarried female informant of twenty-two and a minister for one and an "aunt" for the other). Of course, Mead may have known considerably more than she indicates about any of her subjects, but we cannot tap this source for credibility. On the record it is not all gossip, and Mead herself does not always credit what she hears. However, there is a fair measure of gossip and self-reports and few specific sources other than the subject herself. Knowing almost nothing about the context in which the data were provided, we are in a poor position to judge their reliability.

Whatever the facts may be regarding adolescent sex, Freeman's criticism regarding sexuality goes far deeper than the question of frequencies. In effect, he claims that Mead profoundly misunderstood Samoan attitudes toward sexuality. Some of these criticisms concern sexual morality and its connections with Christianity and pre-Christian Samoan attitudes, others the quality of Samoan sexual experience, the depth of Samoan attachments among sexual partners, and other subtle matters. A number of these criticisms relate to attitudes that are relevant to Mead's contentions regarding stress.

On the question of virginity Mead says the following (1973:98–99):

> The attitude towards virginity is a curious one. Christianity has, of course, introduced a moral premium on chastity. The Samoans regard this attitude with reverent but complete skepticism and the concept of celibacy is absolutely meaningless to them. But virginity definitely adds to a girl's attractiveness, the wooing of a virgin is considered far more of a feat than the conquest of a more experienced heart, and a really successful Don Juan turns most of his attention to their seduction.

This generalization is immediately followed by an illustrative anecdote relating how "the village" laughed at a newly married male "who at twenty-four married a girl who was still a virgin" and "freely related" his "trepidation which revealed . . . although he had had many love affairs, he had never before won the favours of a virgin" (99).

It is not obvious what nuances of chastity and celibacy Mead has in mind in suggesting that the former is revered but viewed with skepticism and the latter absolutely meaningless. Chastity is, of course, connected etymologically and semantically with purity; if this is the emphasis she has in mind, does she mean that Samoans had reverence for "purity" but perhaps were skeptical about its realization? The celibacy distinction is if anything more obscure; perhaps it is its emphasis on the state of being single, or unmarried, that she judges "meaningless." Her claim that Christian notions of chastity-celibacy are not internalized and have little salience can, however, be examined.

Prior to U.S. Naval government and missionary influence, enforcement of chastity was much stricter, in Mead's view; today's girl (ca. 1925) "whose activities are frowned upon by their family is in a far better position than that of her great-grandmother. The Navy has prohibited, the church interdicted the defloration ceremony, formerly an inseparable part of the marriages of girls of rank; and thus the most potent inducement to virginity has been abolished" (1973:274). Mead claims that neither the introduced religious system nor the legal system provide sanctions against premarital sex equal to those of the old regime. This general appraisal is preceded by recognition that "in former times, the head of the household had life and death powers over every individual under his roof" (273). The weakening of powers of enforcement and the banning of the defloration ceremony, Mead argues, have left Samoan adolescent girls with less conflict in engaging in sex than was formerly the case. "Deviations from chastity were formerly punished in the case of girls by a very severe beating and stigmatizing shaving of the head. Missionaries have discouraged the beating and head shaving, but failed to substitute as forceful an inducement to circumspect conduct" (273–74). On internal controls that might inhibit premarital sexuality among Samoans, Mead has little more in the way of explicit declarations. Perhaps her comment that the problems arising from our adolescent sex experimentation might be "greatly simplified . . . if no Puritan self-accusations vexed their consciences" (242) might be taken to imply that she believed that Samoan adolescents were not so troubled. Certainly such comments as "missionary influence which if it has failed to give the native a conviction of sin, has at least provided him with a list of sins" (126) are consistent with this inference.

Though the olden days may have exacted a greater price for premarital sexuality, Mead also argues that the "night dances now discontinued under missionary influence . . . usually ended in a riot of open promiscuity" (1973:138). Did the unmarried adolescent girls steer clear of this "open promiscuity" or simply flout the dreadful sanctions that then existed? On the Samoan attitude toward sexuality per se, Mead characterizes it explicitly as "a natural, pleasurable thing" limited "by just one consideration, social status" (201). As for its place in everyday life she speaks of "the general preoccupation with sex, the attitude that minor sex activities, suggestive dancing, stimulating salacious conversation, salacious songs and definitely motivated tussling are all acceptable and attractive diversions . . ." (148).

A note somewhat discordant with this permissiveness is sounded in Mead's references to the secretive manner in which affairs are carried out by adolescents. Referring to a typical instance of a girl who has just reached the age of fifteen, Mead says that now "all of the adult and near-adult world is hostile, spying upon her love affairs in its more circumspect sophistication, supremely not to be trusted" (1973:68). It is not quite clear what is to be feared from "circumspect sophistication"; is it only embarrassment? A similar reference is embedded in a comment on the ineffectiveness of religious sanctions; here Mead speaks of "being answerable" . . . to a "spying neighbour" (163).

Regarding the internalization of Christian restrictions on sexuality by "young people," Mead says that "western Protestantism with its inseparable association of sex offences and an individual consciousness of sin" has not taken root (1973:164). She says that they have not "been inspired with a sense of responsibility to heavenly . . . decree" and do not consider themselves "answerable to a recording angel" (163). This failure to transmit internalization is attributed to the "native pastors with their peculiar interpretations of Christian teaching" (164). A general "laissez-faire attitude [toward sexuality] has been carried over to the Samoan Christian Church" (232). Pastors "saw no reason why young unmarried people should be pressed to make momentous decisions which would spoil part of their fun in life" (232). Instead of pressing the adolescent to "think upon her soul" the native pastor advises her "to wait until she is older" (232) to join the church.

There are only two references in the entire corpus of field materials that directly speak to the question of internalization, and neither of these is cited by Mead in *CA*. One of these is the previously noted testimony of the white teacher at Atauloma, who volunteered that the pastor's house was the only "safe house" in the village—the only residence for adolescents where sex was unlikely to take place. To a direct question regarding confession and feeling of sin she replied,

"Oh no. They do their best to hide it." When asked if they thought God would punish them if they didn't tell, she replied, "no," and added that "even the taupo is likely to slip." Perhaps most significant is the teacher's comment regarding the pastor, "who is so cynical that he simply refused to admit anyone to communion who is not married." This is the view that Mead adheres to in *CA.*

The second reference comes from an adolescent girl of either fifteen or nineteen known by the pseudonym Lita; this girl, who is listed as a virgin and is one of the few adolescents who is a church member, told Mead that premarital sex is "leaga" (bad). In Mead's view she did not "tafao" and so might plausibly be thought to have internalized the Christian viewpoint. No other informant makes such a statement, and therefore Mead perhaps believed it to be the atypical view of an atypical adolescent who had chosen to be a church member. Indeed, Mead says that she was "very puritanical." Of course, no one offers the contrary view—that premarital sex is "lelei" (good)—either. Indeed, we might well surmise that if asked no one would have expressed such a view; however, even if many had said that it was bad it might still be the case that there was little internalization and that such expression poorly correlated with behavior. Nevertheless, one is struck by the fact that Mead made no such inquiries even after Lita's statement. Perhaps she felt that what she had learned from the white schoolteacher at Atauloma and from her behavioral data made matters so clear that there was no need for further investigation.

What were the behavioral data that might have given credence to her view? There was, of course, the bigamy trial within a month of Mead's arrival in Samoa and the white judge's leniency, which she relates to his understanding that he cannot enforce his idealism on Samoans and to his desire to be popular. Less than a week later there was the palolo-gathering expedition in which Mead interprets the girls' covering their heads as an effort to avoid identification and the clergy as "more intent on the non-appearing palolo." Even earlier, she writes in a news bulletin a disparaging analysis of Samoan religiosity in general, speaking of "old taboos and contemporary Christianity" as providing little in the way of sanctions and thereby robbing the culture of depth and intensity. She speaks of a "diluted Christianity, which consists mainly in the singing of impossible hymns" and "adds no glamour to the life." Clearly Mead was disappointed to have landed for her first fieldwork in a culture that lacked dark malignant spirits and focused preeminently on the "social," in particular on the punctilious performances required for proper recognition of honors connected with titles. Two months later she was to report that "solemnity" was "never of a very reliable depth" during services and to note the rapid transition from Christian hymns to flowers in the girls' hair, the *siva* song, and the dancing "by no means in a puritan fashion." All of this must have seemed a confirmation of her early expectations. The lack of "solemnity" seemed to her a lack of seriousness and a failure to internalize Christian teaching and the rapid transition from sacred to *siva* a clear indication that the connection between sin and sex had not been made.

There was also the evidence on sexual conduct per se of both adolescents and adults that we have noted—infidelity among adults, children born out of wedlock, and illegitimacy. Among the adolescents there was the alleged frequency of heterosexual experience (within the 40% range). Finally, there was the conversation among the adolescents, which was filled with allusions to sexual interests and contacts, though it was always about others that they were speaking. And, as we have seen, Mead was aware of "perpetual joking" on this subject. All of this must have buttressed her conviction that Christian sexual teaching had not been internalized and that indigenous sanctions, weakened by both Christianity and a foreign government, were similarly inefficacious.

As we have seen, five out of six of those living in the pastor's residence and two or more years into puberty are said not to have had heterosexual experience. Since this sample (however representative) is only half of those two or more years past puberty who did not live with the pastor, Mead may at least have felt that these girls were again atypical; in addition, she may have considered that it was the close supervision provided by the pastor and his wife and the sanctions attached to "falling" rather than an internalization of Christian morality or a fear of divine retribution that maintained the attendant celibacy. No doubt instances of "falling" reported to her and efforts at concealment and alteration of rules to provide effective sanctions also contributed to her viewpoint. Unfortunately she never addressed the question why the pastor and his wife were so vigilant.

For earlier times, Mead's fieldnotes indicate such severe punishments for adultery, especially involving a chief's wife, as death and destruction of one's property, though she tends to discount the severity reported. Much of the information on virginity was provided by the wife of an important chief; she says that virgins formerly "left their hair long on top and shaved the sides." This marking of virginity was connected with head shaving if the girl was found to have had intercourse. When this marking was abandoned we are not told, but it certainly does not speak to a long tradition of premarital lovemaking as the Samoans' "pastime par excellence." Mead is fully aware of this, as we have seen in her comment that formerly enforcement of chastity was much stricter but the U.S. Naval government and the church have discouraged the beatings and head shaving and banned the defloration ceremony. All of this might explain an increase in frequency of premarital sex, but the question remains how to reconcile such a tradition with the alleged tolerance of premarital sexuality she reports.

Finally, as we have seen, the ethnographic facts that Mead did collect explicitly refer to a tighter control of adolescent girls than her generalizations suggest. Her field materials, as we have seen, are replete with restrictions on the sexuality of adolescent girls. She records that thirteen-year-old girls could not go where boys were or go out alone and that some adults were "helpless before the 'tafaoing' of their female adolescent wards"; clearly if there had not been restrictions they should not have needed help. Girls in "petting parties" are said to have mistrusted each other, implying that their activities were best kept secret, presumably because they were illicit. It was reported better to use girl go-betweens because they could approach a girl by day; obviously such an approach by a boy was unacceptable. If a boy became angry at a girl, it is said, he could ruin her reputation by spreading the word that she was not a virgin. In the defloration ceremony, banned by the missionaries, members of the family are said to have crowded about the girl who proved to be a virgin and wept over her and thanked her for the honor she had brought them. In "ordinary marriages," informants reported, mothers examined a sheet of white cloth to see if daughters were virgins. Certainly Mead must have understood the pride Samoans had in the proven virginity of their daughters.

Mead's generalizations are, at the very least, often misleading and occasionally discrepant with her data and and even with her explicit understanding. There can be no doubt that Mead knew, both in particular cases and in general, that families sought to curb the sexuality of their adolescent daughters. Thus in a letter to Boas (January 5, 1926), speaking of a particular adolescent, she says, "The girls in her household are not allowed to go out walking in couples with boys." In a later letter to Boas (March 14, 1926) she says, "It is the family and not the community (except in the case of the taupou) which attempts to preserve a girl's virginity . . . and this attempt is usually secretly frustrated rather than openly combated by the adolescent." She was, therefore, clearly aware of family efforts at restraint, and it was her judgment that these efforts often proved ineffective.

5

Who Hoaxed Whom?

Concentrating on Mead's rather hyperbolic and polemical statements about sexuality, Freeman overlooks the qualifications on this freedom that Mead deftly inserts in *CA* and casts about for an explanation of how she could have missed them. This exploration of blind alleys has led him to claim that Mead was "hoaxed" by two young ladies who were at the time of Mead's fieldwork about her age (twenty-four) (Freeman 1989; 1991). One of these, Fa'apua'a Fa'amu, who was an eminent *tāupou*, has survived to this day and was interviewed on November 13, 1987, by Galea'i Poumele, the son of the deceased Fofoa, her alleged accomplice in the hoaxing, and then Secretary of Samoan Affairs of American Samoa. The interview was filmed and became part of Frank Heimans's *Margaret Mead and Samoa* (1988). The published contents are identical with the filmed interview and are presented below as translated by Freeman:[1]

> Question: Fa'amu, was there a day, a night or an evening, when the woman questioned you about what you did at nights, and did you ever joke about this? . . .

> Answer: Yes, we did; we said that we were out at nights with boys; she failed to realize that we were just joking and must have been taken in by our pretenses. Yes, she asked: "Where do you go?" And we replied, "We go out at nights!" "With

90

whom?" she asked, then, your mother [Fofoa] and I would pinch one another and say: "We spend the nights with boys, yes, with boys!" She must have taken it seriously but I was only joking. As you know Samoan girls are terrific liars when it comes to joking. But Margaret accepted our trumped-up stories as though they were true.

Question: and the numerous times that she questioned you, were those the times, the two of you continued to tell these fibs to Margaret Mead?

Answer: Yes, we just fibbed and fibbed to her.

Even if this testimony is accurate in every detail, Mead could not possibly have believed it, for, as we have seen, she consistently maintains that the *tāupou* does not participate in a free sexual life. After speaking of the love affairs of "average young people," she says, "From this free and easy experimentation, the *taupo* is excepted. Virginity is a legal requirement for her" (1973:98). Indeed, she goes on to say that "these girls of noble birth are carefully guarded; not for them are secret trysts at night or stolen meetings in the day time. . . . the high chief guards his daughter's virginity as he guards the honour of his name. . . . The *taupo* may not visit in other houses in the village, or leave the house alone at night. When she sleeps, an older woman sleeps by her side" (100). Clearly, if she had believed her eminent *tāupou* companion Fa'apua'a, she could not have maintained this view of the *tāupou*, and in any case it would simply have added two more cases to her list of those having engaged in premarital sex. Since neither Fa'apua'a nor Fofoa was an adolescent, the sexual experience of these women was hardly relevant to her claims about adolescent girls.

If Fa'apua'a and Fofoa told similar "fibs" regarding adolescent girls in general or in particular, as Freeman reports, and Mead believed them, they would certainly be inconsistent with the nuanced understanding she displays of the sexuality of female adolescents. In spite of her many statements regarding freedom to experiment, as we have seen, she knew that families sought to prevent such experimentation, that the church did likewise, that the daughters of chiefs had no such freedom, and that young adolescents almost never engaged in heterosexual sex. It is therefore demonstrably false that Mead was taken in by Fa'apua'a and Fofoa. Indeed, Fa'apua'a's testimony indicates that she is under the impression that Mead was unaware of any of these restrictions. Otherwise, she would know that what Mead could not have believed her. This is not surprising, since only a very close reading reveals Mead's qualifications regarding "free" sexuality. Samoans generally believe that Mead falsely portrayed Samoa as a land of unbridled sexuality, and they are therefore anxious to discredit her. In my view, the testimony of Fa'apua'a should be understood in this light.

Freeman has described Fa'apua'a as Mead's "principal informant of 1926" (Freeman: 1991:104). However, though many items of information are attributed to specific inform-ants, not a single piece of information in any of the field materials is attributed to Fa'apua'a. Freeman notes that Fa'apua'a and Fofoa are thanked in the "Acknowledgments" of *CA*, and this is indeed the case; their names appear after the statement "I must specially thank. . . ." It continues with the acknowledgment that "their kindness, hospitality, and courtesy made my sojourn among them a happy one; their co-operation and interest made it possible for me to pursue my investigation with peace and profit." A number of those listed were indeed informants as indicated by the field materials, but Fa'apua'a or Fofoa are not among them.

Neither Fa'apua'a nor Fofoa came from the villages in which Mead's adolescents resided and in which she spent most of her time. They were both from Fitiuta, on the opposite end of the island. When Fa'apua'a came to the western portion of the island she stayed with her relative Tufele, an important chief who maintained a household in Si'ufaga as well as in his native Fitiuta and who had provided Fa'apua'a with an important *tāupou* title. Nevertheless, Fa'apua'a had ample opportunity to learn a good deal about the life of Ta'ū, Si'ufaga, and Faleāsao because she had attended high school in Ta'ū village while residing in Si'ufaga (Freeman 1989:1018). Apart from there being no evidence in the field materials that either Fa'apua'a or Fofoa was an informant, it is misleading to say, as Freeman does, that "Fa'apua'a and Fofoa became Mead's informants from January 1926 onward, when they were living in the village of Ta'ū" (1989:1019). Clearly Fa'apua'a was in her own village of Si'ufaga for a considerable part of the time that Mead was in Manu'a. This can be demonstrated by the dates of letters Fa'apua'a sent to Mead from Fitiuta. The first of these is dated January 6, 1926, and indicates that she already had met Mead, so perhaps she was in Si'ufaga in November when Mead arrived and possibly in December as well. She was probably also in Si'ufaga on or about January 26, 1926, when the mother of Tufele arrived with her entourage in Manu'a. Letters follow dated March 25, March 31, April 2, April 10, April 12, April 13, April 16, and April 17, indicating periods when she was not in Si'ufaga.

These letters contain neither ethnographic information nor information regarding sexuality. They are filled with the conventional honorifics, thanks to God, and profuse expressions of affection that are standard for this genre. The dominant content concerns the giving and receiving of valuables that is so prominent in Samoan life; such obligations are aptly referred to as *fa'alavelave*, deriving from a root meaning "to be tangled." In the letter of January 6 Fa'apua'a mentions having sent Mead a pineapple; on March 25 she expresses concern about Mead's illness and notes that she has sent a gift of bark cloth (*siapo*) and urges Mead to ask for anything she might want; she then asks that she be sent some canned salmon and some laundry soap and notes that she has also sent Mead a necklace (*ula*); on March 31 she thanks Mead for what she has sent, expressing disappointment at having received no letter from her and requests flashlight batteries; on April 2 she thanks Mead for having sent a pretty dress, a mirror, and earrings but notes that she has not received any batteries, perhaps because someone else has taken them; on April 10 she tells of a gift for Mead being put together by the chiefs of Fitiuta and then asks for some sugar; on April 12 she says that a mat is being woven for Mead and then asks for 50 cents for a can of corned beef to give to the ladies weaving the mat and for some laundry soap and some sugar. On April 13 she again thanks Mead for the dress, the mirror, and the earrings but repeats that she has not received her batteries; she then mentions having sent Mead a fan and the bark cloth that she had requested; on April 16, two days after the probable date of Mead's departure from Ta'ū, Fa'apua'a thanks Mead for what she has sent and asks for laundry soap for the three ladies who helped to weave the mat for Mead, which was not yet finished. She asks also for two yards of some white material for a dress, adding that she has sent Mead a dress. The final letter, sent while Mead was still in Samoa, is dated April 17, and in it Mead is thanked for a dress and for soap; in a postscript Fa'apua'a asks for some salmon.

Unfortunately, none of Mead's letters to Fa'apua'a are preserved, but there are adequate records in the field materials to indicate that Fa'apua'a and Fofoa accompanied Mead on her trip to Ofu and Olosega from March 8 to March 17, 1926. Though it is not part of the published testimony of Fa'apua'a, Freeman says that Fa'apua'a indicated that it was in March 1926 that she and her friend Fofoa, while traveling with Mead to Ofu and Olosega, were asked about sexual behavior and answered with joking responses suggesting promiscuity (1991:114). (In his 1989 report of the hoaxing, the date and place were not so specific: "when she and Fofoa went traveling with Mead [i.e., to Fitiuta and to Ofu and Olosega]." The latest interview, in May 1993, by Leulu F. Va'a says that the hoaxing occurred over a long period of time: "Thus according to Leulu, it is possible that Meade [sic] had reached her erroneous conclusions over a period of time, rather than instantaneously, and in the manner of Paul's conversion mentioned in the New Testament" [*Samoa Times*, May 21, 1993].)

Mead provides a lively description of this trip in a news

bulletin (XIV, March 24, 1926) completed just after her return. Ofu and Olosega "lured" her "by thoughts of ethnological gain AND the fact that Dr. and Mrs. Lane [whom she had met on Tutuila] were temporarily stationed there. . . . At the last minute, Fa'apua'a, Tufele's taupou, and another Fitiuta girl [Fofoa] came tumbling head over heels into my room and announced they were going with me; I decided that would be expensive but pleasant. So we went out in the broiling sun with a crew of some nine Samoans." Mead goes on to describe the difficulties of the voyage, the approach to Olosega, and a legend regarding some stone figures on a "jagged promontory" as one approaches the island. She tells how difficult life was in Ofu as a result of famine, making it necessary for her to provide food for her own entourage and herself, but apparently she was able to revel "in yeast bread for a whole ten days . . . because there was a bakery in Ofu." Mead tells of her visit with the Lanes and of bathing with them at sunset in a beautiful lagoon. "On Thursday [March 11] I went to the other island, Olesega, in a boat with the Navy men, and while they returned, we, my talking chiefs [Fa'apua'a and Fofoa] and I, stayed the night. But it was a dreary business. Olesega was wrecked by the hurricane." She then describes the acute shortages and how the whole "village was churlish, took our short stay in ill part and tried to hide its poverty stricken shame under vehement protestation. But I found a most excellently old and wise man and got all that I wanted, so we decided to sleep the next night at Sili," which she describes as a charming village where "gracious hosts killed a pig for us and the whole tiny village made merry, while the high chiefs told me anecdotes, illustrated of the days of cannibalism, and a most gaunt and pitiful madman who believes he is Tufele danced and sang for us."

Mead characterizes the whole "malaga" (trip) as "charming":

> My two companions [Fa'apua'a and Fofoa] were my talking chiefs, functionally speaking. They made all the speeches accepted and dispersed gifts, prepared my meals, etc. For this

I bought them each three new dresses. For the talking chief who accompanied his lord need take nothing with him, neither food nor raiment, for he believes and enforces the adage that the laborer is worthy of his hire. But it is all much pleasanter than having a real servant. And these were merry companions. Even when they went to wash my clothes, one carried the clothes, but the other carried her ukelele; and they must play at least a couple of tunes before sitting up in the morning. . . . I dreamed Fa'apua'a had twins, the very night before we left. And that is an 'octopus dream,' could they have gone fishing untold devil fish would have rewarded them. Instead we sailed away on the Man-owah, the Lanes coming also. . . . [The Lanes are] installed in the guest house in Siufaga and have called on me every day this week while I had tonsulitis.

I have included all this detail so that one may judge what Mead found worthy of note. One would think that if on this trip Mead had learned something profoundly important about sexuality that would shape her entire outlook she would have made some mention of it in this news bulletin.

While in Ofu on March 14, Mead sent a handwritten letter to her mentor Franz Boas. It is Freeman's view (1991) that this letter confirms the importance to Mead of the joking "fibs" that Fa'apua'a has spoken of. In this letter, Mead summarizes some of her major findings. Her summary on sexuality follows:

Sexual life begins with puberty in most cases, fairly promiscuous intercourse obtains until marriage, and there is a good deal after marriage. It is the family and not the community (except in the case of the taupou) which attempts to preserve a girl's virginity and this attempt is usually secretly frustrated rather than openly combated by the adolescent. The development of sex interest, of coquetry, etc. is quite sudden and coincident with puberty. The neuroses accompanying sex in American [?]civilization—are practically absent—such as frigidity, impotence, and pronounced perversions. (Then I have detailed information on sexual [?] and beliefs and standards and preferences.) So the sum total of it all is—adolescence is a period of sudden development, of stress, only in relation to sex—and where the community recognizes this and does not

attempt to curb it there is no conflict at all between the
adolescent and the community, except such as arises from the
conflict of personalities within a household (and this is
immediately remedied as I have shown by the change to another
relationship group) and the occasional delinquent—of any age
from 8–50 who arouses the ire of the community. I think I have
ample data to illustrate all these points. As far as I understand
it [?] this is what—that is the sort of thing that you wanted.

This report to Boas, written without benefit of field materials
at hand, presents virtually the same conclusions regarding
sexuality drawn as early as January 6 after what Mead called
five weeks of detailed work. In her report to Dr. Frank R.
Lillie, chairman of the Board of Fellowships of the National
Research Council, which had provided her with a grant for
her study, Mead reports the following on sexuality:

> Along with this institution [testing at marriage of the virginity
> of the *tāupou* and girls of "lesser rank"] there is an extensive
> tolerance of pre-marital sex relations, and the adolescent girl is
> thus presented with a distinct choice. The influence of the
> bilateral social organization is evidenced in the possibility which
> it offers of a change of residence, for if a girl feels she is
> overworked or over chaperoned, she can run away to the other
> side of the family.

A little more than a month later Mead writes to Boas
presenting virtually the same conclusion regarding sexuality:
"The material which I have been able to collect on sex so far
indicates a minimum of sexual activity before puberty and
great promiscuity between puberty and marriage, coupled with
a normal amount of laxity in the married state" (February 15,
1926).

It is therefore clear that Mead's conclusions regarding
sexuality were changed in no way by the alleged fibbing of
Fa'apua'a and Fofoa. However, when Mead sat down with her
field materials to write *CA* she managed to present a much
more nuanced account of adolescent sexuality, excluding
daughters of chiefs, young adolescents, and those living under
the aegis of ministers from the "free" sexuality of others. Such

an account is of course inconsistent with the view that Mead
was duped.

Freeman interprets Mead's February 15 letter to Boas as
indicating that "her planned special investigation" of the
"sexual life of female adolescents" was "only due to begin
after the end of March 1926" (1991:114). Her letter can be
read as indicating this because, after listing "general background" information regarding her "66 children," she says
"for these 66 I will have at the end of the next month, the
following information." Mead then proceeds to list the
background information she is collecting. The next paragraph
begins "There will then remain for special investigation, [The
Samoan adolescent girl's] sexual life and any philosophical
conflicts. These are of course the most difficult to get at,
require the greatest facility in the language and the longest
intimacy." Therefore, Freeman argues, this investigation was
not due to begin until "the end of the next month," that is,
the end of March, when her background material was
complete.

Freeman then claims that Mead was lured away by
ethnographic interests that resulted in trips to Fitiuta and Ofu
and Olosega and that she would have been in deep trouble
had she not obtained the data provided by Fa'apua'a and
Fofoa. This interpretation benefits from Freeman's omission
of one key sentence in the February 15 letter: after speaking
of the "special investigation," Mead says, *"and of course I have
a good deal of material on both subjects already"* (my italics). Clearly,
in her view, these were not topics that she would begin to
investigate only after March. It seems more reasonable to
interpret her statement "There will then remain . . . " as
meaning that in addition to the background material, she has
not yet completed her sexual and philosophical data, which
were difficult to obtain for the reasons she indicates.
Freeman's interpretation benefits also from the omission of
the opening lines of Mead's letter: "I have been taking stock
of the amount of material which I have accumulated and I
think I can now report that my work is going nicely." She

could hardly have thought this had she intended to begin collecting her sexual data at the end of March, for she then would have had only a few weeks to gather it before her scheduled departure in April. What the field materials indicate is that Mead's inquiries on adolescent sexuality continued after February 15. As we have seen, her lengthy interview with "Amigo" on sexuality occurred in March during her stay in Fitiuta and prior to her trip to Ofu and Olosega. After the March voyage and the alleged duping there are entries in the binder dated March 21 and March 24, indicating that her investigation of sexuality continued.

When one compares the data on sexuality that Mead had collected from sources other than Fa'apua'a and Fofoa with the paltry data to which Fa'apua'a testifies, it is evident that such humorous fibbing could not be the basis of Mead's understanding. Freeman asks us to imagine that the joking of two women, pinching each other as they put Mead on about their own sexuality and that of adolescents, was of more significance than the detailed information she had collected throughout her fieldwork.

Freeman asserts that Mead's March 14 letter to Boas, extraordinary in that it is handwritten and sent from Ofu, is consistent with the view that Fa'apua'a and Fofoa provided Mead with such revealing evidence that she felt compelled to write on the spot to report her general conclusions. For the record, it is one of six handwritten letters that Mead wrote to Boas while in Samoa. Presumably it was handwritten because she did not take her typewriter in the rowboat to Ofu. Though Freeman's conjecture that Mead had just learned what she needed to know about adolescent sexuality seems highly improbable, one might still wonder why she chose to write at this time. Judging by the content of the letter, her strongest reason would appear to be concern as to whether Boas would demand that she provide statistical documentation and/or case studies for all of her "children." Referring to her letter to him of January 5, 1926, she says "I await your answer to my airmail letter with the greatest interest as it will partly determine how I will spend the next six weeks. If you want statistics, I'll have to spend sometime rounding them out— likewise if you want case studies for all my children." After describing some of the tools she had constructed to test for variance in her sample and announcing that it is "so little," she says that she will not continue to investigate variability any further unless Boas writes and demands statistics. She then says that she is practically through with her research on her problem and summarizes her results. Perhaps the letter was written at this time and place because it was a Sunday and she had a bit of free time and because she had hoped for a timely reply.

A letter written by Mead to her mentor, Franz Boas on March 19, 1926 informs him that she will "finish up my work here in the next month and leave Samoa on . . . May 10 from Pago Pago." Freeman believes that the announcement of such an early departure is consistent with his interpretation that she obtained crucial information from Fa'apua'a and Fofoa during the trip to Ofu and Olosega. The reasons Mead gives for leaving are "the increasing difficulty of living in Manu'a with too many people [?]quartered at the Dispensary for me to stay there and a famine in native foods."

Lastly, in order to accept the Fa'apua'a account we are required to believe that an eminent *tāupou* joked about her own sexual misconduct, which seems exceedingly unlikely, and that Mead, who was familiar with such joking, in this case failed to recognize it. Perhaps so much attention to an alleged "hoax" that certainly did not succeed is justified on the grounds that no blind alley should be left unexplored for fear that some innocent may mistake it for the royal road to truth.

Notes, Chapter 5, Who Hoaxed Whom?

1. Fa'apua'a was also interviewed by Freeman on November 13, 1987, by Leulu F. Va'a on May 2, 1988, and in May 1993, and by Larry Gartenstein in October 1990 (Freeman 1989:1017 and personal communication). Only the Galea'i Poumele interview has been published.

6

Equivocal Support from a Restudy

Lowell Holmes's 1957 dissertation *The Restudy of Manu'an Culture*, an early attempt to verify the work of another anthropologist, provided valuable corrections of language errors and details regarding social organization in Mead's work. His work has not attracted the attention that Freeman's has mainly because his disagreements with Mead are minor and on the large issues of adolescent sexuality and stress he generally reaffirms her findings.

On the vexed question of female adolescent sexual behavior, attitudes, and restrictions, Holmes in his dissertation has this to say: "Marriage usually comes for men at twenty-five and for women at approximately twenty years of age after considerable amount of sexual freedom without the conflicts that confront the American teen-aged girl. Promiscuity is condemned by the church but winked at by the family. An unmarried girl who finds herself pregnant will face a certain amount of verbal abuse from her family, but the matter is soon forgotten, and the newborn child is welcomed with open arms, without any stigma attached to it" (1957:123). His impression, then, is that both male and female adolescents enjoy considerable sexual freedom that families condone

101

unless the girl becomes pregnant, in which case she is, for a time, subject to verbal abuse. This is certainly in accord with Mead's most hyperbolic generalizations, making no mention of the restrictions that she herself acknowledges or of the efforts at constraint indicated by her field materials. In his 1987 book Holmes reaffirms the findings in his dissertation regarding sexual permissiveness: "The amount of sexual freedom allowed Manu'an girls also may contribute to the lack of trauma in adolescence. Premarital relations were tolerated by the elders and an unwed mother faced only the short-lived anger of her parents and brothers" (1987:106).

In evaluating Holmes's findings we benefit from his straightforward acknowledgment that he found sex to be the "most difficult of all areas of Manu'an culture to discuss" (1957:vii). He adds that "informants who were consulted daily for a period of several months still showed great embarrassment and reticence to speak of sexual matters. Even close Manu'an friends couched their replies to sexual questions in very general terms. No better success was had by my wife when she tried, showing that it is not simply a question of the sex of the investigator. . . . it was never possible to obtain details of sexual experience from unmarried informants . . . " (vii–viii). Holmes adds that Mead might have done better in this regard than he "due to the fact that she was not married when she carried on her study";[1] this conjecture he supports by noting that during two months of his own fieldwork when his wife and child were not living with him he "was in a better position to observe courtship activities," presumably because he was "accepted more as a single man" (viii–ix).

Following the admission of these difficulties, Holmes presents the only informant statements that bear on the question of adolescent sexuality: "The major informant in this study, Lauifi Ili, said on this point, 'while boys are prone to brag about their sex activities, the girls are very close-mouthed and "ashamed"' " (1957:viii). Surely "ashamed" suggests not only some external constraint but possibly even some measure of internalization, which is of course rather contrary to the impression left by Mead. However, one should not make too much of this, since we know that this comment was provided in English because Holmes admirably tells us that his study "was carried on almost entirely with English-speaking informants" (ix). Perhaps the use of "ashamed" was merely meant to convey that discussion of sex was "unseemly," a term that Mead herself uses to describe the attitude toward discussion of sexuality (1973:136). Holmes goes on to say that "other informants stated that girls do not discuss their love affairs with other girls, and the only one who would know of their activities would be their intermediaries"(1957:viii). As he indicates, this is entirely in accord with Mead's account. The 1987 summary of adolescent sexuality quoted above reiterates this position.

What should one make of Holmes's evaluations of female adolescent sexuality? "Considerable amount of sexual freedom" perhaps means more freedom than existed in the United States ca. the 1920s when Mead did her fieldwork. That the church's condemnation is "winked at by the family" suggests a surprising chasm, especially since the church is thoroughly Samoan in personnel. There is not even a mention in this context of the honor of the family connected with virginity. We have, of course, no fieldnotes to supplement what Holmes has published. Nevertheless, his frank account of the difficulty he found in obtaining information on sexuality, the meager sources that he cites, and his complete dependence on a few English-speaking informants do not provide much assurance of reliability. Indeed, the one informant he cites says of the girls that regarding sex activities they are "close-mouthed and 'ashamed.'" If the families so readily wink, why the secrecy and shame? How such data could provide the basis for a judgment of relative sexual freedom one cannot imagine; even less could they provide for an estimate of relative frequency of heterosexual practice. Did Holmes really examine a number of cases of "illegitimacy" and observe that these children were uniformly regarded without stigma?

Surprisingly, Holmes's generalization on sexuality in his 1987 book is "I could not agree with Mead on the degree of sexual freedom supposedly enjoyed by young people on Ta'ū. . . . However there was considerable evidence in the form of illegitimate children and divorces with adultery as a ground to indicate that a fair amount of premarital and extramarital sexuality existed" (1987:103). Perhaps this somewhat cryptic argument connecting adultery and extramarital affairs to "a fair amount of premarital . . . sexuality" rests on the implicit assumption of a generally "loose" attitude regarding sex. Apparently Holmes's current view is that Mead exaggerated the extent of sexual freedom, though his dissertation gives no indication of this, nor does his book present evidence supporting such a position.

On one important point related to the subtle question of attitude toward virginity, Holmes appears to present evidence strongly supportive of Mead's account though in *Social Organization of Manu'a* rather than in *CA*. Speaking of the defloration ceremony of a *tāupou*, Mead says, "If the girl proved not to be a virgin, she was set upon by the women of her village and severely beaten or even killed. But this only happened if she concealed the fact. If she confessed to having lost her virginity the old women cannily substituted a bowl of chicken blood and the ceremony proceeded without any one knowing of the family's shame. With true Samoan courtesy in compromise, the talking chief of the husband connived also at the deception" (1969:96). This report is supportive of Mead's general contention that the whole question of virginity is one of honor and fear of shame rather than abhorrence of premarital sexuality per se, much less Christian principles of morality. Freeman vehemently disputes this evidence on the basis both of principle and enquiry among the "chiefs of Manu'a" (1983a:251). The principle he invokes is the following: "The whole procedure is designed by an intensely rank-conscious society to avoid all possibility of a bridegroom of rank being shamed by a male rival who, if a bride's virginity were not publicly tested, might subsequently claim to have had prior sexual connection with her. It is thus entirely contrary to all expectation that a talking chief, being his chief's active supporter, would connive at having his chief's intended wife deceptively declared a virgin"(251). In 1967 he asked the "chiefs of Manu'a," and "they indignantly rejected Mead's account, saying that if the supporters of a seeming taupou resorted to the unprincipled and highly insulting subterfuge of bringing chicken's blood to a ceremonial defloration they would at once be heavily attacked. They also denied that Mead could have been told of such a practice in Manu'a" (251). Freeman adds that Mead obtained this information "not from any inhabitant of Manu'a but from a Mrs. Phoebe Parkinson" (251) in New Britain in 1929. Freeman indicates that Mrs. Parkinson was hardly a credible informant since she was a half-Samoan sent by her father to a convent school in Apia, the capital of Western Samoa. Educated by nuns, at sixteen she had married a German surveyor named Parkinson, and "two years later she sailed with her husband and child from Samoa to New Britain, never to return"(252).

Though Mead appears not to have been told of such a ruse while in Manu'a, she was told, as we have seen, by a high chief that a girl who is not a virgin should confess to a talking chief so that the defloration ceremony can be omitted. Holmes, however, reports in his dissertation that "informants state that many a girl has been saved embarrassment by the substitution of a chicken bladder full of blood for that normally produced by a broken hymen" (1957:127).[2] Unless Holmes actually learned of such a practice by reading Mead's *Social Organization of Manu'a* rather than from informants and/or Mead manufactured her Manu'an field materials on confession out of whole cloth, Freeman would seem to be mistaken; perhaps his informants were unwilling to admit such a possibility, which would be consistent with their efforts to discredit Mead.

In his dissertation Holmes presents five "aspects of Samoan behavior" in which his views are different than those of Mead;

he generously refers to these differences as "behavior interpreted differently" (1957:222). They are (1) "lack of special-
ized feeling" in human relations; (2) lack of crisis in human
relations; (3) lack of competitive spirit; (4) interpretation of
sex activity data; and (5) importance of the *māfaufau* concept.
On the fourth of these points we have already noted the
substantial agreement with Mead in both the dissertation and
the book combined with an unexplained comment in the
book suggesting that Mead overstated the degree of sexual
freedom—all based on extremely limited evidence. Holmes's
virtue is that in a general way he acknowledges this. The
second and third points will be examined in the next chapter,
where we will note the surprising frequency of agonistic events
in *CA* and the appearance of a number of such events and
traditional practices in the field materials but not in the book.
Holmes is also impressed with this aspect of Samoan life and
cites several useful instances to make his point. A number of
these have to do with an attempt by a chief of Si'ufaga to
make over his land to the Catholic church in 1946. For this
he was deported by order of the village council to Ofu and
eventually settled in Tutuila. In 1948 some priests came to
examine this land with an eye to establishing a chapel;
however, the longboat crews refused to unload the priest's
schooner, and some baggage that had already been unloaded
was "permitted to capsize" (1957:93). "That evening the house
of the Roman Catholic family was stoned" (93). This event is
much like a stoning recorded in Mead's fieldnotes but
unreported in her published account.[3]

Holmes also reports severe beating of children for minor
infractions (1957:102). In his book (1987:106) he says that
he "has never seen an adolescent struck by a parent nor even
severely lectured for misbehavior," but there is such abundant
evidence for such chastisement elsewhere in Samoa that it
would be surprising if it were absent in Manu'a. Doubtless
such actions were less likely to occur in the presence of an
outsider. Holmes also suggests that the punishments for
children were perhaps less severe or at least for rather

different infractions than in the United States. He reports that "no Samoan child was ever forced, as a child might be in America, to finish dinner, to go to bed at a particular time, or to keep from fighting with siblings" (1987:106). What systematic observations support these categorical assertions we do not know. Certainly I have myself seen on more than one occasion corporal punishment meted out for fighting with siblings, though this came only after more warnings than I would have given.

Holmes concurs with Bradd Shore (1982:117) that "there is among Samoans a stress on the maintenance of interpersonal harmony, at least in its external manifestations." This is, of course, entirely in accord with the position of Mead and, for that matter, of Freeman as well. Perhaps it is the blurring of such a preference and ideal with everyday occurrence that makes for misunderstanding. This aspect of the Mead-Freeman dispute is nicely delineated by Schoeffel and Meleisea (1983), who point out that on sex Mead emphasizes practice and Freeman ideals whereas on the expression of emotion and violence Mead emphasizes the ideal and Freeman practice. Mead required easy sexuality and a halcyon Samoa to make her case; Freeman reverses the emphasis so as to produce the maximum contrast.

Finally, in regard to agonistic relations Holmes reports in both his book and his dissertation considerably more rivalry than Mead reports. He finds this rivalry particularly in scholastic performance and among chiefs vying for honor. Again, the evidence for intense scholastic rivalry heavily emphasized by parents and guardians is so well known as to need no comment; it is, however, entirely inconsistent with Mead's assertions regarding the protection of the laggard by the suppression of precocity in every sphere except the dance (1973:116–17). Similarly, the intense rivalry between titled persons has been observed by every serious observer of Samoan political life; though played down by Mead, who stresses the ideal of harmony, it is evident from the field materials that she was aware of it.

The disagreement on the concept of mafaufau (*māfaufau*) seems a storm in a teacup. Mead speaks of individuals' having or not having *māfaufau*, which she translates as "judgment"; Holmes tells us that informants who were apparently asked in English about the term told him that it meant "to think" and were doubtful that it could be translated as "judgment." Holmes then goes on to say that the word is a verb rather than a noun; he, however, seems unaware that in the form *māfaufauga* it means "consideration" or "thought."[4] Apparently "informants" also told him that they did not think the concept "an overly important aspect of individual behavior" (1957:228). "Overly" is exceedingly vague, but perhaps Mead herself would agree that the concept is not "overly" important, since she does not mention it in *CA* and mentions it in a single paragraph in *Social Organization of Manu'a* (1969:81).

On the issue of sexuality it is evident that Holmes's data are far thinner than the meager data of Mead, and though he does better than Mead in admitting how thin, they are plainly inadequate to support his categorical assertions. On agonistic behavior his examples surely help to correct misleading impressions arising from Mead's presentation of preferences for harmony as equivalent to practice, though the evidence is that she knew better. On the largest issues, however, Holmes substantially agrees with Mead. He confirms "Mead's conclusion that it was undoubtedly easier to come of age in Samoa than in the United States in 1925" (1987:103). For the Samoan side of the equation he bases this conclusion on the same theoretical arguments supplied by Mead. Since the household provides more adults than the ordinary American variety, authority and affection are diffused, leading to less stressful parent-child relationships. As does Mead, he accepts this theoretical contention without a shred of evidence, perhaps on the assumption that such an effect is well established; as does Mead, he makes no effort to provide a comparison of households differing in the number of adults present. Indeed, there is nothing in Holmes's work or in that of Mead to suggest that either examined household interaction in any systematic fashion.

Notes, Chapter 6, Equivocal Support from a Restudy of Manu'an Culture

1. Actually, Mead *was* married at the time of her fieldwork, though it is questionable whether Samoans knew this; certainly she was not accompanied by her spouse.

2. I am informed that a chicken has no bladder; perhaps the secum is meant.

3. See Chapter 7, page 117.

4. Holmes says the term is not listed in Pratt (1977), but see Pratt (1977:195).

7

Agonistic Samoa

Freeman argues that Mead, under the influence of Ruth Benedict, portrayed Samoa as far too Apollonian, neglecting the more Dionysian aspects of Samoan life—that she muted the agonistic aspects of Samoan culture and thus produced the impression of a halcyon life that did not exist. Freeman's examples on this point cover both a broad historical record and life at the time of Mead's study. They also span a wide gamut of cultural life, including the supernatural, wars and lesser conflicts, sexual behavior, emotional expression, depth of commitment, and the like.

This criticism, as Freeman notes, was explicitly addressed by Mead in her 1969 monograph *Social Organization of Manu'a*. Freeman speaks of "her supposition of 1969 (voiced after sustained criticism of her findings), that Manu'a in 1925 'might have represented a special variation on the Samoan pattern, a temporary felicitous relaxation,' of the quarrels and rivalries, and the sensitivity to slight and insults that other observers had reported as characteristic of Samoan society both before and after the time of her research" (Freeman 1983b:115; Mead 1969:228). Freeman's quotation of Mead, preceded by "her supposition," suggests that such a temporary relaxation was her only explanation for the discrepancy between her findings and those of some others. There is, however, a second explanation.

Responding to reports on "ethos" in Manu'a by Holmes (1957), Cooper (unpublished discussion cited by Freeman [1966]) and an informant of Copp and Pula (1950) and on the statistics on rape presented by Holmes (1957:228), Mead says, "There is a serious problem of reconciling these contradictions between the mildness, the willingness to gloss over and compromise, which I found in Manu'a, and other records of historical and contemporary behavior. I see at present only two possibilities. Manu'a in 1925 might have represented a special variation on the Samoan pattern, a temporary felicitous relaxation of the quarrels and rivalries, the sensitivity to slight and insults, and the use of girls as pawns in male rivalries." She goes on to mention certain other well-known instances of rapid change (1969:227–28).

Her second conjecture is "that to the young girl, herself either a virgin but not a Taupou, or experimenting quietly with lovers of her own choosing, uninvolved in the rivalries that were related to rank and prestige, moving gently, unhurriedly toward adulthood, the preoccupation of the whole society may have seemed more remote than they would have appeared from any other vantage point. *And this is the vantage point from which I saw it*" [my italics]. I was alone, very slight and smaller than the Samoan adolescent girls. My subject of research called for my spending the largest proportion of my time with them" (1969:228). It is impossible to tell from the field materials if this claim regarding time is correct. Certainly a great deal of material regarding adolescents, as well as virtually all of the ethnographic material, was obtained from adults. Even if it is on balance correct, the amount of time spent with adults including high chiefs makes the claim of "little" Margaret and the children's perspective rather implausible.

Freeman rejects the "felicitous relaxation" conjecture on the grounds that it was a "particularly turbulent period, with deep and widespread disaffection among the Samoans of both Tutuila and Manu'a" (1983b:118). He cites as evidence various manifestations of a Samoan social movement known as the Mau, or "rebellion." For example, Governor H. F. Bryan spoke in 1926 of April 1920 as "a period of unrest" that had "a very disastrous effect on the material prosperity of the islands" of American Samoa (118). In Western Samoa in 1928 the Mau culminated with "sailors and marines from two New Zealand cruisers" arresting "some 400 Samoans," and with the "fatal shooting by police of eleven Samoans, including the high chief Tupua Tamasese Lealofi, who were participating in a procession of protest" in Apia (118). In 1926, with Mead still in Manu'a, "an article appeared in *The Nation* discussing 'abuses and evils' in American Samoa" and drawing "attention to a letter that 344 Samoan chiefs had addressed to the President of the United States in 1921." Freeman notes that in the same year "seventeen chiefs and orators were imprisoned for (as reported in *The Nation*) 'conspiring to kill the high chiefs who had signified their loyalty to the Governor' " (118).

Freeman caps this account of turmoil with evidence pertaining to 1924, when three high-ranking Manu'an talking chiefs, "in open defiance of the government of American Samoa, formally conferred the title of Tui Manu'a on Christopher Taliutafa Young" (1983b:118). A high Samoan chief who was acting district governor participated in the ceremony marking the installation of the new *tui manu'a*. These events created a crisis because the Americans had outlawed the *tui manu'a* title in 1904 as "royal in nature and therefore inadmissible under the Constitution of the United States" (119). The governor of American Samoa summoned the *tui manu'a* and the three talking chiefs to the Naval station in Pago Pago. "Their actions," he said, "smacked of conspiracy" (119). The high chief Sotoa, who was serving as district governor, was "held to be primarily at fault, was suspended from office and the newly installed Tui Manu'a was detained in Tutuila." The three talking chiefs remained defiant and told the governor they were "dissatisfied to the death" with his "interference in the affairs of Manu'a" (119).

However one may reconcile this state of affairs with the idea of "felicitous relaxation," our task is to examine Mead's published account and her field data with reference to the agonistic and nonagonistic qualities of Samoan life. Our question is what she said she observed and how this account is related to her characterization of Samoan life.

The notion of a "felicitous relaxation" was not a view that Mead adopted only after criticism. *CA* is full of examples indicating that Mead regarded the Samoa that she observed as far more mellow and less agonistic than it had been prior to Euro-American influence. She says that "it is only fair to point out that Samoan culture, before white influence, was less flexible and dealt less kindly with the individual aberrant" (1973:273). As we have seen, she says that formerly girl sexual delinquents were dealt with more harshly, with severe beatings and stigmatization. Indeed, Mead argued that "puberty was formerly much more stressed than it is to-day" (275). Menstrual taboos were more strongly enforced: "the unmarried girls and the widows slept, at least part of the time, in the house of the *taupo*. The *taupo* herself had a much harder life" because it was required that she chew the kava root until her jaws ached; should she be found not to be a virgin at marriage "she faced being beaten to death" (275). Male adolescents were subjected to painful tattooing "additionally stressed by group ceremony and taboo" (275). "Today, scarcely half of the young men are tattooed," she reported, and only when they are older and without ceremony. "Even the stern attitude formerly taken by the adults towards precocity has now been subdued, for what is a sin at home becomes a virtue at school" (276). "Formerly it might have been necessary to flee to a great distance to avoid being beaten to death. Now the severe beatings are deprecated, but the running-away pattern continues. The old system of succession must have produced many heartburns in the sons who did not obtain the best titles; to-day two new professions are open to the ambitious, the ministry and the *Fitafitas*" [soldiers] (274).

Continuing in a similar vein regarding feuds, wars, cannibalism, blood revenge, and sanctions, Mead argues that "new influences have drawn the teeth of the old culture" (1973:276). "The intensity of local feeling with its resulting feuds, wars, jealousies and conflicts [in the case of intermarriage between villages] is breaking down with the improved facilities for transportation and the cooperation between villages in religious and education matters" (274–75). "The prohibitions against blood revenge and personal violence have worked like a yeast in giving greater personal freedom. As many of the crimes which were formerly punished in this fashion are not recognised as crimes by the new authorities" (275–76). "Cannibalism, war, blood revenge, the life and death power of the *matai*, the punishment of a man who broke a village edict by burning his house, cutting down his trees, killing his pigs, and banishing his family, the cruel defloration ceremony, the custom of laying waste plantations on the way to a funeral . . . all these have vanished" (276).

A number of economic changes, Mead argues, have also made life easier. Indeed, the only historical change that she feels has brought some discomfort is that the schools have taken particularly the little girls out of the home "and so tied the adult women more closely to routine domestic tasks" (1973:275).

In contrast with the Samoa of those sterner days, Mead describes the Samoa of her field study (1973:198–199) as a society of

> general casualness, . . . a place where no one plays for very high stakes, no one pays very heavy prices, no one suffers for his convictions or fights to the death for special ends. Disagreements between parent and child are settled by the child's moving across the street, between a man and his village by the man's removal to the next village, between a husband and his wife's seducer by a few fine mats. Neither poverty nor great disasters threaten the people to make them hold their lives dearly and tremble for continued existence. No implacable gods, swift to anger and strong to punish, disturb the even tenor of their days. War and cannibalism are long since passed away and now the greatest cause for tears, short of death itself, is a

journey of a relative to another island.

In spite of Mead's claim to have been in Samoa during halcyon days, *CA* is filled with a surprisingly large number of agonistic and negative events and even a fair sample of emotional outbursts. A listing of statements in *CA* about Samoans that are clearly positive or negative (see Appendix) has 36 positives (35% of relevant statements) and 66 negatives (65%). What is even more striking is that for statements concerning adolescents the sum of positives is only 8 (20% of relevant statements) and the sum of negatives 32 (80%). The impact of this negativity regarding adolescents is mitigated by the labeling of six adolescents and one "midway" as either delinquent or deviant; if all statements connected with these adolescents are removed, positive and negative instances are about equal (8 positive, 9 negative). Most significantly, however, few statements are made about the life of "normal" adolescents.

In the field materials, the sum of positives for Samoans of all ages is 54 (41%) and the sum of negatives 79 (59%), slightly less negative than the book. However, 17 of the positive statements are stereotypic responses to questions about the character of some close relative. Excluding these statements, the figures become 37 positive (32%) and 78 negative (68%), somewhat more negative than in *CA*. For all adolescent the figures are 14 positive (35%) and 26 negative (65%); excluding delinquents and deviants, the figures are 9 positive (41%) and 13 negative (59%). Clearly, both the book and the field materials are predominantly negative. Certainly there is no hint that Mead was quantitatively underemphasizing the negative in either *CA* or the field materials.

As one might expect from these figures, there is a reasonably close correspondence between the mentions of individuals in *CA* and in the field materials with respect to agonistic behavior. One must of course take into account that Mead occasionally attributes acts in such a way as to protect anonymity. This is done almost exclusively when the behavior or attributes would be regarded negatively by Samoans. For example, in the "dramatic story" of Moana, quoted in full earlier, all of the fiery, passionate occurrences, including a violation of incest taboos, are described as exceptional, contrary to common practice and expectation. The fieldnotes indicate that the guilty party was not "Mutu," as in *CA*, but a different matai who is not in the census and has no pseudonym. These same notes also indicate that the relationship was not between uncle and niece but between the *matai* and his "adopted daughter." Judging by her comments in the binder, Mead did not in fact consider the case so unequivocal: Moana claims "that the episode was true but seems [?] uninterested. . . . The matai claims it wasn't, but that she had been misbehaving and was turned over to his care by her mother—and [?] that [Moana's] sister misinterpreted some circumstantial evidence." Mead goes on to say that Moana "certainly has had sex experience—is indolent, sensuous." How she knows the girl has had sex experience we are not told, but perhaps this conclusion indicates that on balance Mead accepted the charges against the *matai*. The postmortem removal of the fetus by the *matai* is also described in the fieldnotes (January 30, 1926) in connection with the sexual intrigue.

Mead notes in the same context that "there was considerable laughing and jesting among the young men as they dug the grave." One may well imagine that this made some impression upon her and that she may have connected it with her generalization about shallow affect and/or the "naturalness" with which death was viewed. She does indeed also note the wail of the mother of the dead woman as they "started to wrap the body," but this she describes as "the conventional long drawn out mourning wail." Perhaps another example for Mead of shallow affect revealed by response to death is the following account in a news bulletin: "X [a *matai*] has come to send a wireless message that his daughter was dead. . . . he stayed the two hours and we engaged in slow sorrowful converse until he got interested in discussing the glorious days when there was a Tui Manu'a and he lost both grief-stricken mien and chiefly dignity in the enthusiasm with which he demonstrated, with the help of tin cup, the top of a powder box and wash basin, the elevenfold Kava ceremony of the Tui Manu'a."

However close the correspondence in reports of agonism between field materials and the book, there are some notable examples in the field materials that are not included in *CA* and, had they been included, would have appeared anomalous. For example, as we have seen, the young man who furnished her with so much sex information said that he knew "of two bluebeards, one killed three wives." If one credits this account, perhaps not all the "teeth of the old culture" had been drawn. Again in the fieldnotes Mead says that "the young men of Siufaga laid waste the taro plantation of Lumā, then their own faded and died and they had to have a kava confessional of sin to cast off the curse." She does not tell us what the occasion for this altercation was, and nothing like it is mentioned in *CA*. Similarly in a news bulletin Mead says that she "argued with members of the Aumaga on the advisability of burning down what is left of Ofu, because the people of Ofu stoned the meddlesome pastor of Tau out of the village." All of this violence and threat of violence, apparently of recent or even current vintage, challenges the impression that Mead has emphasized.

An early news bulletin from Tutuila mentions her observing a court case involving a schoolgirl who had bitten off another's ear. The mother of the girl who had been bitten "rose and demanded vengeance declaring that Suli was her only child and that she would rather die than have her lose her ear and also than have the perpetrator of the crime go so lightly punished." There is also evidence of the ordinary quarrels within families that all observers of Samoan village life have noted. For example, Mead was told by the high chief Tufele that "[X] has no guest house because of a quarrel in the family. Later there was a great deal of commotion over this, the young unsuccessful rival to the title tried to build a house on the *malae* sacred to the house of [X]" (fieldnotes, typed

March 22, 1928).

The Mau receives scant mention in the field materials and none in the book. In October 1925 Mead writes in a news bulletin that the secretary of native affairs told her that "Ufuti, the country chief whose guest I was to be, was one of the intelligent chiefs of the island and one of the few who had remained loyal to the government in the rebellion of four years ago. (That was an insane procedure fostered by an unstable officer and a scheming carpetbagger.)" Perhaps Mead's assessment of the affair was based on her belief that it was instigated by outsiders. Like her evaluation of sexual matters, this opinion regarding the Mau came after very little time—and in this instance while she was still in Tutuila. In addition her information and evaluation seem to be entirely based on the report of the American official. There is one additional note on the Mau in the field materials, but it is not clear when it was written. It is what Mead calls a "memorandum" and amplifies her remarks in the previously mentioned news bulletin: "in this connection it must be understood that the disturbances of 1920 which might have involved hundreds of innocent Samoans in warfare had been fomented by an insane Naval officer with grandiose delusions and [a] civilian named Green who was in close touch with the Ripley family who took a prominent part in the artificially fomented rebellion." Also a part of this memorandum is a note on a much-discussed murder in American Samoa and the subsequent trial and execution of the accused (see *New York Times*, March 14, and March 18, 1926; *The Nation*, April 1926): "Sam boy gambling dispute (several years ago) youth bested him in love as well; went vill[age], got gun, returned shot successful oponent; tried hung. Murder nephew Ufuti of Vaitogi whose household I was adopted." Mead was certainly in a position to have obtained this account from Ufuti or his family, though there is no previous mention of the event. Her account is, however, quite consistent with newspaper accounts except that these make no mention of prior rivalry over women. Mead would, of course, have reminded us that this was believed to be the only murder committed in American Samoa since it had been under U.S. authority.

There is the somewhat discrepant account in a news bulletin of the dispute between a "high chief" and a commoner and involving also "Tufeli" (Tufele); one of the participants, it is not clear which, "was determined that Tufeli shouldn't speak at all, and still Tufeli is the highest chief in Tau and he had to be polite to him. . . . your r-r-r-r-oyal h-h-h-iness, sh-shs-shut u-p-p he would blurt out dancing about in his impotent rage." This rage is not at all what one might expect from Mead's account, which so strongly stresses decorum, though it has been widely observed by others. In the very same passage Mead tells us that "Tufeli, who has been district governor for years, has passed, as they say. He got drunk and sassed the Judge and now he is suspended for six months." This passage, like the one that precedes it, gives a rather different impression from the emphasis that prevails in *CA* when the subject is anger.

Freeman is critical of several of Mead's statements regarding rape that he argues are wrong, especially the statement that "the idea of forcible rape or of any sexual act to which both participants do not give themselves freely is completely foreign to the Samoan mind" (1983a: 93, 104, 249). The statement is said to have come from a Mead article of 1938, but what is meant is 1928.[1] Considerable evidence is provided by Freeman indicating that, as is noted by Holmes, rape has been not at all uncommon in Samoa. Again, though Mead's statement is plainly wrong, it does not reflect her actual understanding of the situation. In fact what she says in *CA* is "Ever since the first contact with white civilisation, rape, in the form of violent assault, has occurred occasionally in Samoa. It is far less congenial, however, to the Samoan attitude than *moetotolo*, in which a man stealthily appropriates the favours which are meant for another" (1973:93). "Less congenial than *moetotolo*" seems to have been transformed to "completely foreign," and because it occurred so close to the time of fieldwork, the alteration cannot be attributed to fading or smoothing out of memory.

There is only one mention of rape in the field materials, and that occurs in the binder and refers to the two cases we have seen earlier. No mention of either of these cases appears in *CA* or elsewhere. Mead might well have defended her failure to present these data on the grounds that rape was uncommon or perhaps that she wanted to protect the reputation of her informants and the villages she worked in. Nevertheless, these rapes are surely discrepant with the general impression she conveys. Presented with these facts, the reader might well have wondered how carefree female adolescents were.

One of Mead's strongest arguments on behalf of a halcyon Samoa, particularly for adolescent females, is that adults negatively sanctioned precocity and thus competition between children except "in singing, leading singing or dancing" (1973:116). Here Mead cites the "dreaded accusation, 'You are presuming above your age,'" (*tautalaitiiti* = to be impudent). This is indeed a term commonly applied to both adults and children when one wishes to chastise them for behavior inappropriate to their status, but, as many observers have noted, there are many activities in which competition is not only expected but vigorously encouraged and supported. Two of these in addition to dancing are athletic competitions and scholastic performance. Though Mead chose not to mention these, it is clear that she knew of the scholastic competition. In a letter to Boas (November 29, 1925) Mead notes that "2 girls were recently taken away because their mothers were angry that they did not win prizes in the examinations set by the missionaries each year." Such occurrences remain commonplace. Had they been emphasized, the atmosphere would have appeared considerably more agonistic.

Because Mead requires a halcyon Samoa for her argument of a less stressful adolescence, we are therefore entirely prepared for her failure to report cases of rape, violence, revolution, and competition that the field materials indicate she was aware of. But what of the surprising number of cases she was aware of? And what of the surprising number of negative events noted both in her field materials and in *CA*? It seems likely that this frequency reflects what she actually observed. In both instances it appears that she was drawn to observe and note events that were dramatic and the object of interest and conversation for herself and her informants. Indeed, she herself used the word "dramatic" in describing the "amours" of Moana.[2] Had Mead genuinely been engaged in an inquiry as to whether Samoa presented a less agonistic environment for adolescents than the United States she would, of course, have felt constrained to collect evidence in such a fashion that all kinds of events had an equal chance of observation and recording. Moreover, she would have required a similar sampling of American life. And even if the study were to be less rigorous and more impressionistic, one would still not wish one's impressions to depend on a selection biased by dramatic events. Whatever the actual guidelines were for her selection, Mead certainly encountered and knew of conflict and violence that she did not report; but even what she did report might well have been used to argue the opposite of her case had that been her inclination.

Notes, Chapter 7, Agonistic Samoa

1. Incorrectly quoted as "forcible" (p 249); it should be "forceful" (see Mead 1928:487).

2. I am indebted to Max Yeh, a scholar in comparative literature, for raising this question and providing a reasonable answer.

8

Lessons for Us All

Should a reader without any personal knowledge of Samoa have doubted the reliability of Mead's work? Regarding sexual experience, she claims that it is rare for both partners to be inexperienced; as she puts it, "I knew of only one such case, where two children, a sixteen-year-old boy and fifteen-year old girl, both in boarding schools on another island, ran away together. Through inexperience they bungled badly" (1973:150). This claim implies that she had a sufficient sample of liaisons and knowledge of sexual experience to judge that the one such case that she knew of was rare. Given that the book provides no such evidence, one might have been doubtful, and consideration of the quantity of intimate data such a judgement required should have reinforced this doubt. Of course, as we now know from the field materials, she had nothing like such detailed data. In addition, her contention regarding the failure of the young couple implies that she knows that their sexual experience was unsatisfactory and that this was due to their both being inexperienced. This would be an extravagant claim even about a couple one knew intimately from our own society, never mind a couple from a different society whose language one had just begun to understand.

If this implied omniscience did not strain credulity, the

claim of knowledge that follows it should surely have alerted even the most gullible. On the very next page Mead asserts that sexual artistry is so widespread that there is "no frigidity, no impotence, except as the temporary result of severe illness, and the capacity for intercourse only once in a night is counted as senility" (1973:151). Not only does she not provide us with any data to support such a claim, but it seems hardly credible that such data could have been collected in any reliable fashion. As we now know from her field materials, she had one informant who told her that he knew of no female frigidity or male impotence and who intimated to her that a particular sexual repertoire was standard operational procedure. That this same informant told her that "girls will always tell other girls how awful first night was, and make derogatory comments on lover's skill," for whatever it is worth, is not reported by Mead in *CA*, perhaps because it is discrepant with her claim of virtually universal sexual skill.

A reader knowing nothing about Samoa might have also noticed that comparisons crucial to Mead's argument are never made. For example, she asserts that the size of the residential unit is a key factor in producing a less troubled adolescence, but she does not compare the adolescent experience of girls from larger and smaller families. Similarly, she makes no effort to compare the adolescent experience of girls who remain chaste under the watchful eyes of the pastors and their wives with that of girls she claims are left free to engage in liaisons. Surely such comparisons would be appropriate to any genuine voyage of discovery. Lacking such comparison, one should have been skeptical of the reliability of her argument.

Furthermore, there is the general problem of the paucity or absence of supporting data for her argument. In *CA* she gives no indication of how she knows about the sexual experience of her subjects; she offers not even anecdotes to convince us that there is no guilt connected with premarital sex; she provides no evidence indicative of the Samoan view of natural functions of the body and sexuality; nothing illustrates a lack of "idealism"; there is no investigation of "philosophical perplexity"; and, of course, no effort is made to construct a metric for comparing Samoan and American adolescent experience.

These are by no means all the defects that might have been observed by those innocent of all things Samoan, but surely they are sufficient to suggest that no knowledge of Samoa was required to have been skeptical of Mead's claims. How is it, then, that Mead's work became so influential? How could anthropologists and other eminent scholars have largely ignored such blatant defects? How could generations of university professors have included *CA* as required reading for students? How could such a flawed work have served as a stepping-stone to fame?

It is perhaps useful in answering this question to begin by admitting that I am among the countless scholars who failed to attend to the faults of Mead's work that required no knowledge of Samoa. So apparently is Derek Freeman, who tells us of his original "unquestioning acceptance of Mead's writings," and tendency to "dismiss all evidence that ran counter to her findings" (1983a:xiv).

I believe that there are two basic reasons for the general failure to recognize Mead's extensive methodological faults. The first of these is ideological: We wanted Mead's findings to be correct. We believed that a more permissive sexual code would be of benefit to us all. More important, her findings were a coup for the proponents of the importance of culture vis-à-vis biology. This perspective supported solving human problems by social change, whereas the emphasis on biology insisted that our problems were rooted in human nature and therefore ineradicable. In addition, the cultural emphasis was a tool against racism insofar as it diminished the linkage between biology and behavior. The fact that the message was delivered in a skillful and charming manner and that we had inherited a vision of a South Sea Island paradise enhanced the acceptability of findings that were ideologically palatable.

The second reason for the failure to note the many deficiencies in Mead's work derives from a pervasive problem of cultural anthropology as a discipline. From its inception, its practice has often been profoundly unscientific and positively cavalier in its willingness to accept generalizations without empirical substantiation. It tends to make little use of logic and mathematics in expressing relationships and seldom employs reasonably well-defined concepts. It therefore often produces propositions that are untestable. Relationships and concepts tend to be so ill-defined that they provide too much "wiggle room"—opportunity to claim that whatever test has been offered to falsify a claim has missed the intended meaning.

There were certainly social scientists, even in the 1920s, who were aware of the requirements of science and who demanded that their students adhere to them. Indeed, Mead herself was quite aware of these standards, as she indicated in a letter to Boas written from the field January 5, 1926. After almost two months of work in Manu'a, she asks Boas for advice as to how to proceed:

> Ideally, no reader should have to trust my word for anything, except of course in as much as he trusted my honesty and averagely intelligent observation. I ought to be able to marshall an array of facts from which another would be able to draw independant conclusions. And I don't see how in the world I can do that. Only two possibilities occurr to me and both seem inadequate. First I could present my material in a semi-statistical fashion. It would be fairly misleading at that because I can't see how any sort of statistical technique would be of value. But I could say "fifty adolescents between such and such ages were observed. Of these ten had step-mothers and five of the ten didn't love their step-mothers, two were indifferent and three were devoted. Fifteen had had some sex experience, five of the fifteen before puberty etc."[1] All of which would be quite valueless, because whether fifty is a fair sample or not could be determined only on the basis of my personal judgment. And saying you don't love your step-mother, or that you rebel against your grandfather but mind your older sister, or any of the

thousand little details on the observation of which will depend my final conclusions as to submission and rebellion within the family circle, are all meaningless when they are treated as isolated facts.

The paragraph ends on a plaintive note to the effect that she doubts "whether the Ogburns [William Fielding Ogburn, a noted sociologist then at Columbia known for his emphasis on statistical rigor] of science will take any other sort of result as valid." As we now know from the overwhelmingly favorable reception of Mead's work, either there were not very many such "Ogburns of science" or they were so pleased with her findings that they were willing to overlook the work's scientific failings.

Though there are many anthropologists of today as ignorant of statistics as Mead was in the 1920s, her statement that the fairness of a sample of fifty depends upon her "personal judgment" is an egregious error. Of course, a "fair sample" means one that is representative of some population. To choose such a sample, one employs a process of randomization. In fact, Mead made no effort to choose a random sample even of the female adolescent population of Manu'a or of her three villages; as we have seen, some of her statements claim that she sampled all of the adolescent girls of the three villages, but in fact she did not. Furthermore, the question of the adequacy of a sample of fifty depends not on anyone's whim but on a well-established statistical principle. Large samples obviously provide more accurate estimates of a population characteristic than do small ones; the size of the sample required can be calculated for any prescribed degree of accuracy (see Blalock 1972:214–15). Whether this technique was widely known in the 1920s I cannot say.

The second possibility considered by Mead in her letter to Boas for meeting the canons of science was to

> use case histories, like this. "[X] is a girl of 12 or 13. . . . She is just on the verge of puberty. Her father is a young man with no title and a general reputation for shiftlessness. . . . She regards her playmates as so many obstacles to be beaten over

the head. She has no interest in boys whatsoever, except as extra antagonists.". . . But to fill such case histories with all the minutiae which make them significant to me when they are passing before my eyes is next to impossible. And the smaller the details become, the more dangerous they become if they are to be taken just as so many separate facts which can be added up to prove a point. For instance, how many other little girls carry babies all the time, and how many other mothers go visiting. Facts which possess significance in one case but which are mere bagatelles of externality in another would have to be included in each case history or they would not be comparable.

Mead goes on to say that she has a lot of detailed data. "But how to use it? If I simply write conclusions and use my cases as illustrative material will it be acceptable? Would it be more acceptable if I could devise some method of testing the similarity of attitudes among the girls, in a quantitative way. . . . I wouldn't feel any wiser after collecting information in that style but maybe the results would be strengthened."

What Mead is claiming is that she is quite confident of her conclusions even though she has not done any formal sampling, and therefore the only reason to do such sampling would be to convince others. In addition, she claims a kind of insight based upon context and judgment that can never be justified by a presentation of observations. Her colleagues, then, must either except her judgment or not. Of course, even if one concedes that an observer may know more than she can demonstrate, one might still contend that a concession might more readily be made if one were presented with the observations that are available. Mead is asking to be excused from collecting and presenting a fair sample and supporting her conclusions with case histories. What she wants is permission to present data simply as "illustrative material" for the representativeness of which one will simply have to take her word.

Mead need not have worried, for Boas turned out not to be one of the Ogburns of science. On February 15, 1926, he wrote her as follows:

I am very decidedly of the opinion that a statistical treatment
of such an intricate behavior as the one that you are studying,
will not have very much meaning and that the characterization
of a selected number of cases must necessarily be the material
with which you have to operate. Statistical work will require the
tearing out of its natural setting, some particular aspects of
behavior which, without that setting may have no meaning
whatever. A complete elimination of the subjective use of the
investigator is of course quite impossible in a matter of this kind
but undoubtedly you will try to overcome this so far as that is
at all possible. I rather imagine that you might like to give a
somewhat summarized description of the behavior of the whole
group or rather of the conditions under which the behavior
develops as you have indicated in your letter to the Research
Council and then set off the individual against the background.

Boas adds that Mead might follow the "methods that is used
by medical men in their analysis of individual cases on which
is built up the general picture of the pathological courses
that they want to describe." To be fair to Boas, he does not
quite give Mead carte blanche to present only illustrative
material, but he is totally unconcerned with the question of
the representativeness of her samples, and of course he offers
no criticism of her comment on sample size. His acceptance
of the context argument as the basis for not having to justify
by empirical example calls to mind the twice-told tale of the
"Belfish Bushmen." As Hans Reichenbach told the tale in his
course on the philosophy of science, an anthropologist just
returned from field work among the Bushmen was asked by
a physicist colleague what was the most striking thing about
them. He replied that their one extremely salient characteristic
would be very difficult to convey to someone who had not
experienced Bushman life. The physicist, a man of many parts,
replied that he appreciated the difficulty but urged the
anthropologist to make an effort nevertheless. "Well," the
anthropologist replied, "the characteristic that is most pronounced is how belfish they are." When the physicist asked
for clarification, the anthropologist repeated that it would be
very difficult to explain the term to one who had not

experienced Bushman life. "Perhaps," the physicist politely said, "it would help if you would provide me with some examples of things the Bushmen do that are belfish." "Yes," said the anthropologist, "that is easily done; for example, one day I desperately needed an ax to cut down some trees, and when I asked a Bushman who was making no use of his ax if I might borrow it, he absolutely refused. On another occasion I saw a Bushman who had much more game than he could consume refuse to share any of it with another Bushman who had none." "Well," said the physicist, "I don't want to leap to conclusions, but 'belfish' seems to mean something very like our 'selfish'!" (It should, however, be noted that real anthropologists have claimed that real Bushmen are exceedingly generous; recently the limits of this generosity have received greater emphasis.) "By no means," said the anthropologist. "Without having experienced Bushman life it is impossible to understand how profoundly different the two terms are." "Yes, indeed," said the physicist, "I can see how that might be so; perhaps, however, you could provide further help by giving an example in which a Bushman does something that you would call 'belfish' but we would not call 'selfish.' " "That I cannot do," said the anthropologist. "The difference can only be known to those who have experienced Bushman life!" With the blessing of Boas, the "father of American anthropology," Mead provided a charter for nonempirical justification: "If you weren't there with me, you simply can't really understand. Therefore you may take my word for things or not, as you like."

What the field materials and *CA* actually indicate is that on a number of matters in which observational interpretation might well depend on context, Mead's generalizations rest on virtually no observations whatsoever. As we have seen, Mead conducted no inquiry among her adolescent girls regarding guilt or fear of divine retribution for violating sexual mores; she seems to have relied on the comments of one white schoolteacher. One girl told her that premarital sex was bad, and she chose not to report this; perhaps she believed that such a comment was atypical, but perhaps she was wrong. One might conceivably believe that premarital sex was "bad" and still not feel guilty; perhaps the remark meant only that one feared for one's reputation if found out. The point is that Mead gives us no reason for having confidence in her judgment on this important point.

On somewhat less subtle matters such as Mead's contentions about the absence of frigidity and impotence, as we have seen, she had but one informant. Surely this would not have been claimed had she been required to present supporting observations. Of course, the experience of sexuality and the attitudes surrounding it are indeed subtle matters. We may demonstrably know more about them than we can clearly explain, or we may think we do and be mistaken. It might therefore be thought that Mead's meager empirical support for her contentions is connected with the subtlety of her subject matter. This, however, is certainly not the case. Mead's quite prosaic monograph *The Social Organization of Manu'a* is plagued by the same practice of almost never telling how things are known. For example, in an account of so-called fine mats (*'ie tōga*), she asserts a number of alleged equivalences; for example, "a fine mat is a two guinea payment; four large tapas a mere two pounds." "One fine mat is the virtual equivalent of any of the following: one large pig, four large tapas each four to five yards in length, ten small tapas, forty floor mats, ten bed mats, a roll of sennit three feet long and eight to ten inches in diameter" (1969:74). Clearly, we are dealing with no subtle matters here, yet not a clue is given as to how this is known. Was it told her? Did she get these equivalences by asking for equivalences? Did she observe any such transactions? I was unable to find any evidence for these assertions in the field materials. Since the perceived quality of fine mats varies greatly depending on a number of technical features such as the fineness of the weaving, decoration, size, and so forth, as well as its history, Mead's equivalences seem greatly oversimplified at the very least. Except for rather low-quality fine mats sold in the market, I have never observed their being used in market exchange; there are occasions that require the presentation of one or more fine mats, and, according to my observations, no one substitutes currency or other valuables. Unfortunately, we do not know if Mead observed anything different.

A number of objections to my critique immediately spring to mind. In the first place, it seems to impose a rather positivistic mold on all anthropological inquiry. To this objection I say that I have no such intention; however, if one is not going to do science then one must avoid the impression that it is being done. One may not claim that a theory—for example, that there is a biological basis for adolescent stress—has been tested and disproved by a counterexample. If, in contrast, one is to do a creditable humanistic inquiry, then it ought to be filled with the sensitive observations that will help readers to see why one thinks as one does. Occasionally Mead does meet this test, and doubtless this is the genuine strength in her work.

A second set of objections is that this was Mead's first fieldwork, that she was only twenty-four at the time, and that today there is a much higher standard of fieldwork and argument. These particular objections were widely stated in the numerous reviews and commentaries on Freeman's critique, and one notes at the outset that they are frequently combined with a stout defense of Mead's work. It reminds one a bit of the folktale about the lady who borrowed someone's pot and failed to return it; when called upon to give it back she said, "In the first place, I never borrowed it, and besides the handle was broken!" Be that as it may, Mead's age and inexperience are irrelevant to my inquiry because I am not concerned with an appraisal of Mead; my interest is an appraisal of the work. I am perfectly content to let others judge whether her later work was done with greater skill. The question of the time at which the work was done is of concern to me, however, because it raises the question whether my critique has any relevance to anthropology as it is currently practiced. Here, in my view, lies the genuine wider significance of the Mead-Freeman dispute. That Mead's seriously flawed work, which is filled with internal contradictions and grandiose claims to knowledge that she could not possibly have had and is so weakly supported by data, could have survived and formed the foundation for an illustrious career raises substantial doubt regarding improved standards of research. Though it would be inappropriate to cite current research that has all the scientific failings of Mead's work, I have many such examples in mind. I can also bring to mind some excellent works that are not lacking in scientific rigor and others that frankly present themselves as more humanistic inquiries rather than making unwarranted claims. Finally, I do not gainsay the achievement in anthropology of some greater measure of understanding, both scientific and humanistic, than existed in the days of Mead. I do, however, insist that her scientific stance and her unscientific practice are far too prevalent even in these times. That a person of such conspicuous talent could have produced such a flawed work and that it was so widely accepted and praised by so many should serve as an object lesson to us all.

Partially confirming the currency of my critique is the fact that virtually none of the numerous reviews of the Mead-Freeman controversy point to the profoundly unscientific nature of her work. This failure is doubtless to some extent attributable to attempts at damage control or "spin doctoring," but some of the comments indicate a rejection of scientific practice on the basis of a naive understanding of the nature of such practice. One example comes from a review by one of our best Samoan ethnographers, Bradd Shore, whose 1982 monograph on the Samoan village of Sala'ilua is filled with valuable insights on Samoan culture and personality. Shore (1983) perceptively notes that a number of Freeman's criticisms of Mead suffer from what Schwartz (1983:919) has called a "maximally contrasting" bias—a tendency to say that things are precisely the opposite of what one's opponent has said that creates an equally misleading impression. Shore helpfully points out a number of other instances of this bias.

Unfortunately from my perspective, he regards Freeman's misleading and oversimplified rejection of Mead's claims as an exemplification of "Popperian" science (1983:943):

> What is wrong, in the end, with the kind of absolute, formal refutation that is the hallmark of Popperian science and that informs Freeman's book is that it pretends the "facts" of human existence operate like some bloodless, mindless machine according to the strictest principles of Aristotelian non-contradiction. And yet human life is riddled with contradiction, with colliding impulses and incompatible values. Simply bringing to bear on a statement evidence that is contradictory is not in the human sciences sufficient to disprove that statement.

Shore seems unaware that there is nothing illogical about people having "impulses" and/or values that lead them sometimes to do one thing and sometimes another, about wishing to do something and feeling that one ought not to, about being torn between conflicting impulses and/or values. It is only in applying the word "contradictory" to such instances that one might be led astray. Logically, "contradictory" means "mutually incompatible," but there is nothing incompatible about "contradictory" impulses and values. It is therefore not the fault of logic that Freeman sometimes oversimplifies the human experience. Shore's "bloodless, mindless machine" is set forth as though it defined the proper range of the application of logic: clearly, there is no more justification for mutually exclusive arguments regarding humans than there is for such arguments regarding "machines." Logically contradictory evidence refutes an argument. Constructing arguments that are capable of refutation is the hallmark of science. I cannot think of a polite term for arguments not admitting of refutation; perhaps the phrase "not even wrong" is all the condemnation that is required. Shore's antiscientific bias is capped by his statement that "Freeman seems to have redesigned human nature to satisfy the requirements of positivistic methodology." There is nothing in scientific methodology that demands that our impulses and values be configured so as never to push us in opposite directions. One might as well claim that science denies, a priori, the opposition of physical forces on the grounds that they are "contradictory."

In fairness to Freeman it must be said that one of Shore's criticisms of his work is plainly unfounded and the result of a misunderstanding. Shore asserts that he "cannot concur with the blanket assertion that Samoans' 'engaging affability,' their smiling or politeness, is always 'in reality, a defensive cover for their true feelings,' a mask for aggression, or depression, or hostility" (1983:939). After providing an example of a difficult social situation in which a chief is being criticized, Freeman says, "As these examples indicate, it is usual, especially in demanding social situations, for Samoans to display an affable demeanor which is, in reality, a defensive cover for their true feelings—to be as they themselves put it, 'smooth on top but whirling beneath' [*e manino i luga' ae vivili i lalo*]" (1983a:217). Clearly, Shore's "always in reality" is not what Freeman said or meant. Furthermore, the Samoan saying plainly indicates that Freeman is perfectly aware—as are Samoans—of the ordinary complexity of human experience.

My describing Shore as a gifted ethnographer despite all this may seem a vindication of antiscience, but I do not believe this to be the case. All of us develop understandings of behavior without knowing how we have come to them; some of these we cannot articulate or may articulate in ways inconsistent with our practice. Nevertheless some of these understandings may be demonstrably correct; of course, some may also be demonstrably incorrect. For example, any ordinary native English speaker can tell with considerable accuracy when someone is telling a joke. To tell how one knows is of course much more difficult, and perhaps few of us could provide a precise rule for making such a judgment. It is therefore not at all necessary to practice science to be good at understanding human behavior. The difficulty in the practice that Shore advocates is that it does not require the careful testing of insights by means of observations. Therefore neither he nor the reader should feel confidence in his insights until they have been tested. I know that his assertions are often reliable because I have tried some of them out; occasionally, too, I have noticed that an unconfirmed suggestion of his is mistaken. When such a gifted observer cannot articulate precisely how he knows something, he may of course still tell us what he thinks he knows and present us, so far as he is able, with the observations that confirm his insight. If there are no such observations, he may of course still be right, but neither he nor the rest of us can tell.

While plainly recognizing that Mead's emphasis on "obedience, gentleness and cooperation" (1983:936) is one-sided, Shore attributes this to "the notion of cultural configuration—being worked out in its early phases by Benedict," which may have led her to simplify her observations "so as to conform to a single dominant theme." But such an explanation of her error overlooks the fact that this simplification neatly fits her argument; the opposite emphasis would hardly be consistent with a more tranquil adolescence. The same is also true of her misleading emphasis on sexual freedom. In both cases we know that she knew better, and had she wished she could easily have made the opposite case. It may be better for the reputation of Mead and anthropology to defend Mead's misleading statements on the grounds of commitment to a high-flown concept, but the convenience of her misleading statements seems to have a simpler explanation. Those who still believe that Mead's misleading generalizations are the result of looking for dominant themes might note that one of these generalizations is that "neither poverty nor great disasters threaten the people to make them hold their lives dearly and tremble for continued existence" (1973:198). Mead experienced both a destructive hurricane and a heavy storm on January 12, 1926, that resulted in enormous damage to both homes and crops. Such storms are by no means infrequent. Surely her generalization here cannot be attributed to looking for patterns, but it is consistent with the requirement of a halcyon Samoa. The storm is, of course, not reported in *CA* or elsewhere.

A similar antiscientific perspective is manifest in the review of the Mead-Freeman controversy provided by Annette B. Weiner (1983:909). Weiner has a number of perceptive things to say about Samoan culture. In particular, she points out how Freeman fails to take account of Samoan sensitivities regarding sexuality, religion, and history and therefore asks us to accept Samoan accounts at face value that ought reasonably to be interpreted in the light of these sensitivities. But she condemns Freeman for holding the view that "there is one Samoan reality, and there are no contradictions to be found in understanding an individual's perceptions, negotiations, and interactions" (913). She cannot mean that mutually exclusive things are true; perhaps she means by "contradiction" something like what Shore means.

Weiner later says that "the notion that there is a single 'true version' of history, genealogy, or oral traditions comes from a Western positivist position in which the scientist believes in the existence of ultimate truth." It is difficult to imagine a scientist who would use the term "ultimate truth," but, be that as it may, Weiner's intention seems again to be to remind us that we must be careful in accepting what Samoans say about such matters as their history. Noting the comments of the anthropologist Malama Meleisea, Weiner says that "different versions of genealogies, oral traditions, histories, and events are told and accepted and the 'truth' depends on situations such as one's relationship to others and the political relationship of one's residential village to other villages" (1983:914). Certainly it is correct that Samoans like all other peoples construct accounts of events often with an eye to their social use. Some of these accounts, to speak plainly, are patently untrue and even self-contradictory. That Samoans twist the truth like the rest of us in no way indicates that they are lacking a sense of *the* truth. If there is any need to demonstrate this, I might note that Samoans are as quick to utter the epithet "liar" (*pepelo*) as any people I have known and are not unaware of efforts to construct accounts of history to serve some political end.

Insofar as one is considering propositions that are in principle verifiable, it makes no sense to speak of multiple truths, though it has become fashionable in contemporary academia to do so. Of course people may have different experiences, depending, for example, on their social status or a host of other factors. If one wishes to call these different experiences different "truths" one may do so, but these different truths are not logically contradictory. Observers may even see—in a literal sense—the same event differently depending on their physical positions, but there is nothing logically contradictory in this either. Freeman may say that he has refuted Mead on some point when in fact he has not. This is not the fault of positivist science or logic. Often both Mead's statements and Freeman's have enough ambiguity in them that it is impossible to know just what they mean; in such instances it is of course impossible to speak of verification or of contradiction.

The ambiguous notion of multiple truths has become a charter for the idea that "anything goes," that you have your truth and I have my mine, and ultimately for a rejection of empirical verification. In its most egregious form this approach holds truth to be merely a label employed by competing interest groups to sanctify beliefs useful to furthering their ends. From this perspective, evidence for propositions is of little interest; competing claims are seen simply as furthering competing ends, and the demand that propositions be stated in a manner capable of verification is vilified as ethnocentric positivism and doubtless a tool of some ruling class. In such a climate it is not surprising that the profoundly unscientific nature of *CA* has hardly entered the debate.

No doubt a more scientific climate in anthropology in the 1920s and afterwards would have reduced the probability of Mead's having engaged in such an unscientific inquiry and made it unlikely that her work would have been so widely accepted. But the acceptance of anthropologists like myself, who knew full well the requirements of ordinary scientific practice, points to the power of ideology in our response to ideas. Unfortunately, I was not alone in this mistake. In a splendid modern book on biology and behavior that addresses the very heredity-environment issue at the core of Mead's work, the biological anthropologist Melvin Konner has this to say: "Mead was one of the greatest of all social scientists, and if she had become the first such scientist to win the Nobel Prize in Medicine and Physiology (she could have been cited for instance, for her contributions to pediatrics and psychiatry, as well as for her almost single-handed formulation of our present, flexible concept of human nature), the choice would have done credit to the Swedish Academy." (1982:107).

In view of Konner's demonstrated practice of thoughtful science, there can be no question that he knows how it ought to be practiced. To be fair to Konner, it must be said that he does not specifically attend to *CA*, and the work of hers that he directly considers is *Male and Female* (1949). Furthermore, he implicitly acknowledges her inattention to quantification and "exactitude"; writing in praise of the work of the anthropologists Beatrice and John Whiting, he says of the former: "She is one of the most quantitatively oriented of anthropologists, and may be said to have built an edifice of exactitude on the foundation that was laid by Margaret Mead" (1982:112). What Konner likes about Mead's work is her emphasis on a flexible concept of human nature, in the case of *Male and Female* the flexible nature of what were often called, rather ambiguously, sexual role models. Today the word "gender" would likely replace "sex" here, signifying the very flexibility that Mead championed. But *Male and Female* does draw on Mead's Samoan findings, and even if her later work in New Guinea was less subject to criticism, it seems a flimsy basis for deciding on a view of human nature, especially if it is a view one favors! A Nobel Prize in a field of science seems a bit extravagant for championing a cause without scientifically acceptable evidence. One can, however, learn a good deal about males and females, the flexibility of human nature, and the complexity of interaction between heredity and environment from Konner's thoughtful work. I have cited his essentially unqualified praise of Mead only to warn us of the power of ideology to anesthetize our critical faculties.[2]

Sophisticated practitioners of the "natural" sciences rather than the "unnatural" ones might argue that ideological predilection could hardly diminish *their* capacity to judge things as they are. And so as a final example of the blinding power of such predilections I have a current example from the writings of the eminent Martin Gardiner, whose powers of analysis and clear explication many of us have long admired. Writing in the *Skeptical Inquirer* on what he calls "The Great Samoan Hoax," he uncritically accepts everything that Freeman has to say. He speaks of "irrefutable evidence . . . supporting the claim that young Mead was indeed the gullible victim of a playful hoax" (1983:131). As we have seen, it is not even irrefutable that Fa'apua'a and her friend even tried to hoax Mead, that such a hoax, if it did take place, fooled her, or that it would have mattered if it had. The question is not whether some young unmarried persons had sex but whether it was in some sense permissible. He claims that Mead thought Samoans' sex lives were unrestrained, but, as we have seen from analysis of the text, this is simply not true. In his zeal to make the hoax charge stick, Gardiner provides an account of what Fa'apua'a said that includes things she never said, judging by the published texts; he has her saying without quotes "yes, adolescents had complete sexual freedom, moving stress-free from childhood to adultery." As we have seen, this is not what Fa'apua'a claims in the text that Freeman has published. She claims only that she and her friend Fofoa joked about their own sexual exploits. Freeman maintains that she made similar claims about the adolescent girls but has published no text of these remarks or how they were elicited. No one has claimed that Fa'apua'a said anything about life being "stress-free from childhood to adultery." That would hardly be fit content for joking remarks! Furthermore, Gardiner distorts Mead's argument by claiming that she "was convinced that Samoan adolescents never suffered the anxieties and torments of Western teenagers" because their sex lives were unrestrained. A greater degree of sexual acceptance and permissiveness was but one of the factors that Mead considered as contributing to a less stressful adolescence, and the word "unrestrained" is inconsistent with her understanding. Of course, Gardiner could not have known that there was not a single word in all of Mead's field materials indicating that Fa'apua'a was any kind of informant. Nor was he knowledgeable enough about Samoa to recognize that Mead could not possibly have believed Fa'apua'a's alleged account because she would then have had to maintain that the *tāupou* was not chaste.

As Gardiner makes clear, he is glad to see Mead undone partly because, as he has shown in previous works, she supported beliefs in "occult" phenomena such as the notion that "the earth is being observed by extraterrestrials in flying saucers" (1983:131). But, more important, he strongly supports Freeman's call for a more "interactionist" anthropology with greater attention to biological factors. Gardiner links this biological emphasis with establishing universal human needs and with a less relativistic perspective in evaluating cultures. Whatever merit there may be in these views of Gardiner, they have certainly dimmed his usual inquiring, skeptical perspective. Ideology can make dupes of us all.

Notes, Chapter 8, A Lesson to Us All

1. It is curious that this hypothetical example has a considerably lower rate of sexual experience than her actual sample and a much higher rate of experience prior to puberty.

2. Following the critique of Freeman, Konner notes in his *Why the Reckless Survive, and Other Secrets of Human Nature*, a sequel to *The Tangled Wing*, that Mead's "characterization of Samoan life hasn't weathered the decades very well" (1990:156–157).

9

Conclusions

Freeman contends that Mead depicts adolescent heterosexual experience as under little adult constraint and as commonplace. Clearly, there are lines enough in *CA* and other works of Mead to justify such a claim. However, a close reading of *CA* and examination of the field materials demonstrate that Mead was well aware of a number of limitations on the sexual life of Samoan adolescent girls. These acknowledged limitations were connected with age, rank, and residence in a pastor's home. Furthermore, there is considerable evidence in the field notes and even some in *CA* indicating specific restrictions on female adolescents.

As for the actual experience of heterosexual relations, Freeman has pointed out that slightly less than half of Mead's adolescent sample had had any such experience, and approximately the same figure may be derived from the field materials. Because the evidence regarding sexual experience for any particular person is so thin, it is difficult to judge its reliability. It was obtained in haphazard fashion from the subjects themselves and from other adolescents, children, adult females, and adult males, including *matais*. In a number of instances there is no indication in the field materials of how the information was obtained. Surely no great reliance should be placed on the accuracy of these findings. (Perhaps, as the anthropologist Tim O'Meara observes in the Heimans film, her figures are too high, since none of her adolescent girls seem to have become pregnant!) Whatever the actual occurrence of premarital sex may have been, clearly it was unacceptable for females and perforce clandestine, and Mead certainly knew this. There were doubtless those in the villages in which she worked who were eager to impugn the character of others by rendering accounts of their sexual escapades. At the same time, since premarital sex was unacceptable, families and their daughters have sought to conceal it. Any reasonable and unbiased observer would acknowledge both of these tendencies.

Though some of Mead's statements imply the acceptability of premarital sex for unmarried adolescent females, we know that she knew better. Where her views and Freeman's may really differ is on the deeper attitudes toward sexuality. Mead, as we have seen, argues that fundamentally Samoans think of sex as "natural" and "pleasurable" and are not vexed (as we are) with "Puritan self-accusations." We have seen how thin her written field materials are on the question of guilt connected with sexual offenses. Nevertheless, it is certainly her claim that in contrast to conjectured "us," Samoans could violate the sexual norms of the Christianized Samoa of the 1920s without internalized guilt; no doubt she sees this as contributing to less stress among Samoan adolescents. In addition, she holds that Samoan boys and girls are concerned about being caught out in violation of rules rather than fearful of God; as she puts it, "had the young people been inspired with a sense of responsibility to a heavenly rather than an earthly decree and the boy or girl been answerable to a recording angel, rather than a spying neighbour, religion would have provided a real setting for conflict" (1973:163–64).

Precisely where Freeman stands on these difficult points is not clear from his writings. He speaks of a "cult of virginity" (1983a:234–35) as though that contrasted with Mead's view; but, as we know, whatever misleading statements she made Mead clearly knew that Samoans prized virginity. As she puts it, "To be a virgin's first lover was considered a high point of pleasure and amorous virtuosity" (1973:146; see also 98). As for the relatives of the girl, she acknowledges that it is to their credit and honor including her groom "if she proves to be a virgin, so that the girl of rank who might wish to forestall this painful public ceremony (public testing of her virginity) is thwarted not only by the anxious chaperonage of her relatives but by the boy's eagerness for prestige." He does not really attend to Mead's contrast between Samoans' view of sex as natural and pleasurable and "our view of it as unnatural." Mead notes in *CA* that "there is no privacy and sense of shame" with regard to the "normal processes of evacuation" (1973:137). Certainly any American observer is likely to have made a similar observation and perhaps even been embarrassed at the solicitous attention given to one's own excretory activity. Perhaps Mead would also point to what she calls "minor sex activities" such as "suggestive dancing, salacious conversation, songs" and sexually tinged "tussling," which are regarded as "acceptable and attractive diversions" (148). Freeman uses the term "prudish" in referring to the "Christian society of Samoa in the 1920s" (1983a:238). Insofar as the term means "excessive or priggish modesty or decorousness," "prudish" might well be taken as in opposition to these contentions. However, I do not think that Freeman would take issue with any of these particular contentions.

What follows this characterization makes clearer what he has in mind but unfortunately raises certain other difficulties. What he says is that in the "Christian society of Samoa . . . sexual intercourse between unmarried persons was held to be both a sin and a crime . . . " and that this is "confirmed by cases in the archives of the high court of American Samoa" (1983a:238). He seems, then, to be calling "prudish" a society that regards such intercourse as a sin and a crime, whatever its other attitudes toward sexuality. He contends that the view of "fornication" as a sin and a crime arose "when a puritanical Christian morality was added to an existing traditional cult of virginity" and "this religiously and culturally sanctioned ideal

strongly influenced the actual behavior of adolescent girls"
(239).

The difficulty here is that the "cult of virginity," which as
Freeman says is pre-Christian, has virtually nothing in common
with a "puritanical" aversion to sexuality and pleasure. It is,
rather, as is widely acknowledged, an important element in a
system of honor; in this system males strive to deflower as
many virgins as possible while at the same time standing guard
over the virginity of females of their own family. This aspect
of male exploit is neatly characterized by the well-known
legend of Vaovasa cited by Freeman (235); in it the hero
Vaovasa deflowers ninety-nine maidens and commemorates
each with a large stone, building a wall to celebrate his
triumphs. A rival hero prevents his hundredth triumph by
deflowering his intended victim first and hurling at him a
package containing her hymenal blood (235). No one disputes
that this traditional double-standard system persists. Christianity has certainly added the notion that males also ought
not to engage in sex before marriage, and, as we have seen,
Mead knew that males as well as females were expelled from
church schools if they were found to have violated this
prohibition. However, if a male is caught it is unfortunate,
and he must take his punishment if it cannot be circumvented,
but a deflowered female is a dishonor to her family and a
source of triumph to her conqueror. Christianity has no more
succeeded in eliminating sex as male exploit in Samoa than
it has elsewhere.

The fact that sex between unmarried persons was then as
now punished according to custom or law simply does not
speak to the question of internalization and certainly says
nothing about "puritanical" or "prudish" attitudes toward sex.
Judging by Mead's field materials, she certainly did not have
sufficient data to back up her claim that those who engaged
in illicit sex were free from a sense of guilt or, as she put it,
"individual consciousness of sin" (1973:164). Unfortunately,
Freeman's evidence of effective enforcement of sex prohibitions simply does not speak to these subtle questions. It does,

however, speak to the difficulties that plagued adolescent girls found to have engaged in illicit sex. *CA* gives us no sense of the severe beatings suffered by adolescent girls thought to have broken the rules and thereby brought dishonor to the family. How much of this Mead was aware of we do not know, but it is certainly inconsistent with the easy sexuality that she often asserts.

Perhaps any one-word characterization of some aspect of a way of life such as "prudish" is bound to be misleading. But just as Mead is aware of the restrictions on premarital sexuality, Freeman equally understands that Samoans are hardly exemplars of priggish modesty. It is easy to find examples in which Samoans censor speech and action that concern sexuality in a context where they are held to be inappropriate, but it is equally easy to cite the recitation of bawdy tales such as the one that Freeman himself tells. A common response on the part of an audience to such a tale of exploit is a throaty exclamation of "avi," which means to be "sexually attractive or seductive" (Milner 1966:39) and which in this context is like the Spanish "¡Que hombre!," ("What a man!"). Freeman's misleading characterization in spite of his profound knowledge and experience of the other side of Samoan life seems a perfect example of what one of his reviewers calls his "maximally contrasting" bias. In summary, Mead has skillfully left us with an impression of less restriction on premarital sexuality than she knew to be the case and with a higher frequency of such intercourse than is indicated by her data, whereas Freeman has left us with an impression of extreme limitation of sexuality by concentrating on the system of sanctions and church doctrine.

On one well-defined empirical issue connected with religion and sexuality Mead and Freeman appear clearly to disagree, and that is whether pastors admitted unmarried Samoans to communion and membership in the church. In *CA* Mead says of her adolescent girls that they "defer church membership until they are older. . . . One of the three villages boasted no girl church members. The second village had only one,

who had, however, long since transgressed her vows. . . . In
the third village there were two unmarried girls who were
church members" (1973:164). As we have seen, the practice
of not admitting the unmarried to communion was first
described to Mead by a teacher at Atauloma before she even
went to Ta'ū, and this teacher related it to the cynicism of
the pastors concerning sexual abstinence. We know also that
she reported in a news bulletin on February 9, 1926, that two
subjects "being married have now become church members."
An additional note on church membership is contained in
the binder:

> If church members fall often—the time of probation for
> reinstatement is lengthened. Only [X] fell, not [Y] and [Z].
> Sometimes the church members only scold and suspend the
> person from communion for 2 or 3 months. The best time for
> a girl to become Ekalesia [member of congregation] is when
> she is grown up 18 or 19 and a boy when he is 20 or so. If
> younger brother desires very strongly to become Ekalesia they
> may—still they are too young.

Unfortunately, it is not clear who provided this information;
however, the information coming just before this entry was
provided by two young men aged twenty-two and sixteen,
respectively; perhaps they are also the source for this
information. The binder also indicates that one seventeen-
year-old female adolescent had "been a church m[ember] for
three years. Some say she has fallen but this is not so—at
least officially." Clearly Mead had the information to indicate
that church membership was not always delayed till marriage.
However, as Freeman points out (1983a:185), Mead says that
"no one becomes a church member until after marriage"
(1929:269). But, as we have seen, this is flatly contradictory
with the data in *CA* and her field materials. This seems simply
another instance of Mead's smoothing out the findings to
make her point. What would appear to be a sharp qualitative
difference in understanding turns out to be a quantitative
difference. Mead's field materials indicate that she was told
that membership in the congregation was delayed until

marriage to avoid the chastity problem; in addition, she was told that it was best for a girl to become a member when she was grown. She claims in *CA* that the numbers indicate that this was indeed generally though not uniformly the case; unfortunately, there is nothing in the field materials which speaks to the quantitative claim.

Freeman calls Mead's claim regarding church membership for adolescent girls a "misrepresentation of a crucially important aspect of their [Samoan] social and religious lives" and one to which "Samoans take the keenest exception" (1983a:185). He quotes an eminent Samoan, To'oa Salamasina Malietoa, as saying in 1967 that this was "a most mistaken story" and as having added "that throughout Samoa girls were prepared for church membership from as young as 10 years, with many adolescent girls becoming full members of the church, or Ekalesia, from 15 or 16 years of age onward" (185). Surveying all the girls of the village of Sa'anapu between the ages of fourteen and twenty-two Freeman found that 82 percent were members of the congregation (185). The importance of the issue stems from Mead's argument that not encouraging adolescent girls to join the church is an example of a religious setting "of formalism, of compromise, of acceptance of half measure" (1973:164). Such interpretations and adaptations of Christian doctrine by native pastors are said by Mead to "have made it impossible to establish the rigours of western Protestantism with its inseparable association of sex offenses and an individual consciousness of sin" (164). In the 1929 article Mead precedes her claim about not admitting adolescents with an account of the preaching of a Samoan pastor that neatly conveys her sense of Samoan adaptation of Christian principles: "Preaching on David's sin with Bathsheba, after picturing in vivid and orthodox style the enormity of that sin and David's repentance in sackcloth and ashes, [the pastor] added: 'But why did David make all that fuss? The Lord was right there waiting to forgive him all the time.' " No such account of any sermon is provided in *CA* nor is there any evidence of it or any other sermon in the field materials. No place or time or indication of the language used in the sermon is provided. Though it is clearly impossible to judge it's authenticity, this sermon certainly conveys Mead's sense that Samoans were not overburdened by a sense of sin and preferred to emphasize God's readiness to forgive.

Freeman tells us that in addition to his information from Salamasina and his survey of Sa'anapu, he "was assured, by both male and female informants who had been adults at the time of Mead's researches and well remembered the years 1925–26, that an identical system—with the recruiting of unmarried pubescent girls to church membership . . . had also existed in Manu'a at that time" (1983a:185–86). But, as we have seen, in *CA* Mead clearly indicates that some of her adolescent girls were members of the congregation. The real question is whether it was discouraged for the reason that Mead alleges. Freeman argues further that since nine of the twenty-five adolescents listed in Table I of *CA* were resident members of a pastor's household "they would have been either actual or prospective members of the Ekalesia" (186). Doubtless every Samoan is a prospective member of some church if not an actual member; however, there is no reason to believe that such residents were necessarily members of the congregation. Finally, Freeman quotes a number of researchers on the strong role of religion in Samoan life: Holmes is quoted as saying that Samoans were "almost fanatical in their practice and observance of Christianity" and Governor Bryan as reporting in 1926 that Samoans were "innately and intensely religious," with "family prayers in the morning and evening in every Samoan home" (184). No one, including Mead, would deny such punctilious adherence to the form of Christianity. Her claim is that in spite of rigid adherence to the forms of Christianity, Samoans have adapted the meaning and emphases of Christianity to their own ends. Whether membership of adolescent females in the congregation was discouraged we do not know, but were it so, it would be consistent with Mead's argument.

Mead does indeed say, as Freeman notes, that Samoans were "without the doctrine of original sin" (1973:277). And Samoans would certainly "take immediate exception, pointing out that sinfulness, or *agasala* (literally, behavior in contravention of some divine or chiefly ruling and so deserving of punishment), is a basic Samoan concept antedating the arrival of Christianity. . . . " and "that the doctrine of original sin contained in the scriptures is something with which, as converts to Christianity, they have long been familiar" (1983a:188). What Freeman says here is indisputable but in my opinion does not at all come to grips with Mead's meaning.

Mead's "original sin" is surely meant in the sense of John Calvin (1960:251–52):[1]

> Original sin, therefore, seems to be a hereditary depravity and corruption of our nature, diffused into all parts of the soul. . . . For our nature is not only destitute and empty of good, but so fertile and fruitful of every evil that it cannot be idle. Those who have said that original sin is concupiscence have used an appropriate word, if only it be added—something that most will by no means concede—that whatever is in man, from the understanding to the will, from the soul even to the flesh, has been defiled and crammed with this concupiscence. Or, to put it more briefly, the whole man is of himself nothing but concupiscence.

To what degree the missionaries pressed this view on the Samoans is beyond the scope of this inquiry, but I doubt that there are any observers of life in Samoa who would characterize Samoans as holding this gloomy view. Sex as "natural and pleasurable," as Mead puts it, contrasts reasonably with the dread of "concupiscence" that often accompanied the Puritan spirit. Given a reasonable interpretation of Mead's meaning, there is no contradiction between Freeman's clearly correct observation that many Samoans certainly know of the idea of original sin and Mead's contention that they were "without the doctrine."

Though context seems to me to make it quite clear what Mead meant regarding "original sin," her comments in *From the South Seas* (1939:xiv–xv) reinforce our understanding. Speaking of the Manus of New Guinea, she says "like our Puritan ancestors, [they] assume that man's fundamental drives are immoral, and that man must be broken to fit the accepted form regarded as the good life." Following this she says, "The Samoans have no idea of original sin—no idea that social forms necessarily thwart the demands of the human body or the wishes of the human heart." Certainly a good case can be made that Samoans have not bought the gloomy notion that "man's fundamental drives are immoral," but it is more than dubious that they are unaware of the conflict between human drives and social forces; in any case, it is clear that in speaking of knowledge of original sin Mead certainly does not mean that they are ignorant of the events in the Garden of Eden.

Was Mead in Samoa during particularly halcyon days? Certainly she is correct that the missionaries had discouraged the beating and head shaving that were formerly the lot of female adolescents found to have engaged in sex. The existence of such severe penalties does not fit easily with her contention of a very permissive attitude toward adolescent female sexuality. She also notes that the Navy and the church had interdicted the defloration ceremony required for marriages of girls of rank, and there is little doubt that the interdiction had had some effect. She is probably also correct that menstrual taboos were formerly more strongly enforced and that a *tāupou* was much more likely formerly to be beaten to death if she was found at marriage not to be a virgin. "Feuds, wars, cannibalism, blood revenge," and severe sanctions had been mitigated; in these ways, at least, the Samoa of Mead's day was more peaceful and less punitive than formerly.

Freeman is of course quite right to point to the Mau as evidence of considerable turbulence, and we have noted that Mead makes no mention of it. Perhaps this is an example of her smoothing out the data to make her case. The field materials indicate, however, that her Naval informants had left her with little doubt that the episode was of little importance. That she was so cocksure of her understanding of the event after two months in the field and apparently without inquiry among Samoans is certainly to be criticized, but it is quite possible that she did not consider the Mau indicative of great turbulence.

The quantity of agonistic events contained in *CA* and additional agonistic events in the field materials suggest that Mead's experience in Samoa was closer to the mark as understood by others than her published generalizations. Perhaps a fair judgment is that Samoa ca. the 1920s was more peaceful than formerly but not nearly so peaceful as Mead would have us believe. While she may have smoothed out or eliminated certain discrepant agonistic and violent events, she did, however, fill her field materials and *CA* with events of this nature that attracted her attention. If we attend to the agonistic events that appear in her field materials but not in print and the preponderance of negative events and generalizations in both the materials and the book, there is no need to conjure up a "temporary felicitous relaxation" of tension. The Samoa that Mead actually observed seems entirely consistent with other roughly contemporary and subsequent observations. Reports about the period prior to colonial rule and the predominance of Christianity suggest considerably more violence and sterner sanctions than Mead indicates.

Holmes's restudy of Manu'an culture was a genuine voyage of discovery. By careful investigation and with adequate empirical support he corrected a number of errors (in details) made by Mead. Unfortunately, on the basis of admittedly fragmentary information and totally unsupported conjecture, he has both supported and denied Mead's views on sexuality. In his dissertation of 1957 he maintains that adolescents of both sexes enjoy considerable sexual freedom; in his 1987 book he still speaks of considerable sexual freedom but says that there is less than Mead indicates. Whether or not these imprecise judgments are correct, Holmes has admirably revealed to us how meager the supporting evidence is. Having

far fewer data than Mead, it would have been better had
he not spoken on these matters. Holmes reports substantially more rivalry and competition than Mead, and here
he appears to be on solid ground with adequate data to
support his claims. His judgment in concordance with
Mead that Samoan adolescents suffered less stress in
coming of age than Americans would appear to rest upon
an unsupported impression and the same unsubstantiated
theories put forth by Mead. Anthropology ca. 1987 seems
no more demanding of evidence than that of the 1920s,
though Holmes is much more straightforward than Mead
in revealing what evidence he has.

The claim of Freeman that Mead was duped regarding
adolescent female sexuality is based on the false assumption that Mead was unaware and did not report the
restrictions on such sexuality. The citation of misleading
and hyperbolic statements of Mead has lent credibility to
Freeman's claim. Mead plainly could not have believed
what Fa'apua'a says she told her because she did not
believe there was or claim unfettered premarital sex.
Furthermore, she could not have believed Fa'apua'a
because Fa'apua'a was a *tāupou* and she would then have
had to believe that *tāupou*(s) were not chaste. In fact, she
maintains that they were. As we have seen, not only was
Fa'apua'a unlikely to have been Mead's principal informant, as Freeman reports, but she appears to have been
regarded by Mead as no kind of informant; for there is
not a single bit of information in the field materials
attributed to Fa'apua'a. There are other reasons as well
for rejecting the duping interpretation, such as the fact
that the alleged testimony of Fa'apua'a hardly compares
in detail, never mind seriousness, with the evidence that
Mead had compiled from acknowledged informants including the adolescent girls themselves.

As we have seen, Mead's presentation of both population
and sample size is filled with ambiguity and contradiction.
Understating her population and overstating the proportion

of girls she studied makes her haphazard samples appear more adequate than they are.

Mead's field materials and publications indicate the limits of her competency in Samoan. However, judging by the field materials it is evident that most of her inquiry regarding adolescents was conducted in English. Fortunately for her— but contrary to her claim—a number of the young people spoke fair to excellent English. In addition, she was provided with considerable information on adolescence and sexuality from older informants who also spoke English. However limited her knowledge of the language, it does not appear to account for any substantial errors in her published work.

Mead's impression may well have been that her Samoan adolescent girls were less troubled than American adolescents, but, as we have seen, a quantitative appraisal of agonistic behavior could well have been used to argue quite the opposite. As for Mead's interesting and provocative suggestion that the organization of the family results in a diffusion of affect, she makes no effort to compare size with affect diffusion, nor is there any substantial evidence in the field materials or in the book that bonds really are weak as compared with those in our own society. Where a case of extreme jealousy occurs she discounts it as aberrant and confounds desirable restraint with actual affect. She may well have believed that Samoans never suffer from frigidity or impotence, but as we have seen she had virtually no evidence for such a claim.

This is a serious list of failures, and it of course does not include her demographic distortions and her misstatements regarding language. But does the fault lie in her hunch that adolescent stress might better be understood as cultural rather than biological? I think not. Her belief accounts for the particular slant of her interpretation; she certainly was not going to bend the data to show that Samoan adolescent girls were at least as troubled as those in the States. She was certainly searching for every possible facet of Samoan life that might contribute to a more tranquil adolescence. On the basis of exceedingly limited data she was willing to make extravagant claims regarding the degree of sexual satisfaction enjoyed by all Samoans; in short, she was out to make the strongest possible case for her position.

Certainly Freeman recognizes Mead's tendency not to present evidence that might undermine her position and usefully points to many instances of this. Unfortunately, instead of attributing this to the polemical quality of Mead's work he argues that prior to the publication of Popper's 1966 *Logik der Forschung* (English language edition titled *The Logic of Scientific Discovery*) "the notion of subjecting one's own theories to rigorous testing was unknown" (1983a:60). This is, of course, tantamount to claiming that prior to Popper no one knew that if tests produced data contrary to a theory one was obliged to report it! Popper's contribution was his emphasis on the asymmetry of consistency and inconsistency; genuine evidence against a theory refutes it, whereas evidence consistent with a theory provides no assurance that it will withstand additional evidence. All of this rather high-flown philosophy is neither here nor there, because it is unthinkable that Mead's inquiry constituted anything like "rigorous testing."

Had Mead had the opposite point of view she could, by the same practices, have slanted her interpretations accordingly. Her failure in my view was the result of a number of profoundly unscientific practices. Making her argument in the form of a lengthy discursive essay rather than concisely helped to obscure its logical consequences; as we have seen, she does not recognize that she must show that Samoan adolescence is not more stressful than other periods of life in Samoa. Clearly any claim to validity would require some metric with which to compare stress in the United States with that in Samoa; beyond the difficulty of constructing such a measure, there would of course have been the Herculean task of sampling the United States. Lacking both the measure and the study, she relies on impressions based upon her own experience and the literature of the time, also impressionistic and anecdotal. Mead should have attended to that most scientific of all questions—what evidence she would consider inconsistent with her hypothesis. Without such an under-standing her work may properly be damned with the harshest scientific criticism of all, that it is "not even wrong," for without such consideration the meaning of her claim has not been adequately specified. Finally, she fails repeatedly to supply the observations to support her many generalizations and there is no evidence for her theoretical conjectures about the organization of the family and its effects. In short, if Mead is taken as having done science, she did a bad job of it, and the procedures she employed would have produced unreliable results whatever her hunches.

In part Mead's work is polemical, offering what a colleague of mine has nicely termed "lawyer's arguments." Lawyers, of course, present only the facts that fit their case and seek to cast doubt on points raised against it. So do most of us, in fact, especially in heated argumentation; we nonlawyers have the advantage, however, in that such practice is not required by our profession. Freeman also falls prey to this human failing in summoning evidence regarding the homogeneity of Samoan culture. Citing several experts who emphasize the homogeneity of Samoan culture, Freeman goes on to say that this justifies his "use of pertinent evidence from any of the Samoan islands" (1983a:117). But he knows better than any of us that even neighboring villages in Samoa may differ profoundly in social organization, with some being dominated by chiefs (ali'i) and others by talking chiefs (tulāfale); more to the point, however, neighboring villages may even differ profoundly in the prevalence of agonistic relations and violence. The reason Freeman argues for homogeneity is to make his data from a Western Samoan village relevant to Mead's findings in Manu'a.

All of us who allowed ourselves to be persuaded by Mead that she had found adolescence less stressful in 1920s Samoa than in the United States, and especially those of us who disseminated this finding as though it rested upon something solid, ought surely to be faulted. Doubtless many of us did so because we wanted such findings to be correct. We believed that a more permissive sexual code would be of benefit to all of us. But most important of all, her findings were a coup for the position that culture is more important than biology. Such a finding was supportive of solving social problems by social change in opposition to the position that such problems are rooted in biology; it was peripherally a blow against racism, since it tended to diminish the linkage between biology and behavior. All of these perceived benefits were made especially pertinent because the message was delivered in a charming fashion. Had Mead provided the opposite message we no doubt would have much more readily noted its profound inadequacy. Those of us who went along with the work did so because, for us, she was on the side of the angels and delivered her message so effectively.

Beyond the point-by-point claims on particular empirical issues, does the inadequacy of Mead's work invalidate her grand contention that adolescence was less stressful for Samoan female adolescents in the 1920s than for their counterparts in the United States? Clearly, she did not have adequate data for either place to make such a claim, and her theoretical conjectures, however plausible, are a house of cards completely lacking in verification. Perhaps by some sensible interpretation of "stress" she was correct, but we are far from knowing how such a comparison should be made or even what kind of measure Mead would have thought appropriate to her understanding. Without a definition of stress or a means of comparing it cross-culturally, we cannot know if it was less among female adolescents in Samoa than in the United States. Without knowing this, we cannot know what effects culture and biology have on such stress. In these important matters it is not that Mead is mistaken but that she is "not even wrong." On the more specific question of the degree of sexual freedom for adolescent girls, she leads us to imagine more sexual freedom than exists but at the same time is aware of the actual limitations. An anthropology that on the largest issues is "not even wrong" provides no foundation on which to build genuine understanding. It is, however, invulnerable to refutation, whatever Freeman may think. We should all wish it to be otherwise.

If adolescence was more stressful in Samoa than Mead suggested, does this make it clear that the reasons are biological? Certainly not. More things under the sun may be biological than many of us might like, and certainly we should give the biological devil his due—for, as Tawney has said with reference to material interests, "in the long run, he turns the table by taking his due and something over" (1961:231). Anthropologists' voyages to remote parts of the world should be genuine voyages of discovery and not occasions for designing tracts in support of an ideological position. And all of us should be especially on guard when that position is one that has our sympathy!

Notes, Chapter 9, Conclusions

1. For those who might insist on an earlier source than Calvin, St. Augustine (1872:49–51) says of original sin that "each man, being derived from a condemned stock, is first of all born of Adam evil and carnal and becomes good and spiritual only afterwards, when he is grafted into Christ by regeneration."

Appendix

Evaluative Statements in *CA* and Field Materials

CA

Preface 4

grace and zest and gaiety of the Samoans.   +++

15   "boy taunted by another, who has succeeded   -
him in his sweetheart's favour, grapples with
his rival."

"tale of Losa's [ad] outraged departure from   - +
her father's house to the greater kindness in
the home of her uncle."

23   "These are really simply a series of avoidances,   -
enforced by occasional cuffings and a deal of
exasperated shouting and ineffectual conversation." Punishment falls on oldest child.

25   Boys and even adults vent their full irritation   - -
upon the heads of troublesome children; kids
lashed with palm leaves, stones; stones nine-
tenths gesture; as with dogs.

27   Girls waste hours in bickering.   -

35   "very seldom is he absolutely assured of   -
       getting such a name . . . He has many rivals
       . . . He must always pit himself against them
       in the group activities. . . . he should not be
       too efficient, too outstanding, too precocious
       . . . neither arouse their hatred nor the
       disapproval of his elders."

41   "universal servitude . . . for the children an   -
       hour's escape from surveillance is almost
       impossible."

43   "No Samoan child, except the *taupo*, or the   +
       thoroughly delinquent, ever has to deal with
       a feeling of being trapped."

       "until his noble anger is healed against his   -
       noble child."

51   Timu (ad), daughter Malae's dead sister,   -
       father quarter-caste, "Dancing was an agony
       to her."

       Meta (pre-ad) pushed wall; feeling inferiority.   -

52   Filita (ad): "efficient, adequate."   +

57   Sila (ad) married at sixteen against will to   -
       much older man "who had beaten her for
       her childish ways."

62   "Possessed by a fear of the chiefs, a fear of   -
       small boys, a fear of their relatives and by a
       fear of ghosts, no gang of less than four or
       five dared to venture forth on these nocturnal
       excursions."

63   "Some little girls of fourteen might have   -
       tolerated Luna [midway], but not Selu [ad]."

64   Siva (midway) "vivid and precocious child."   +

"But Siva had proved too much of a handful   -
for her widowed mother."

Maliu (midway): "had a tremendous feeling   +
for all her young relatives."

65   Vina (ad), "a gentle unassuming girl of   +
fourteen."

Flurried anxious child, overconcerned with   - +
pleasing others, docile in chance encounters
with contemporaries from long habit of do-
cility.

68   "But when she is fifteen and her cousin   -
nineteen, the picture changes. All of the adult
and near-adult world is hostile, spying upon
her love affairs in its more circumspect
sophistication, supremely not to be trusted."

86   first attitude little girl learns toward boys is   -
avoidance and antagonism.

(ads) good-natured banter.   +

91–92   recognised cause of a quarrel is the resent-   -
ment of the first lover against his successor
of the same night, for the boy who came later
will mock him.

Girl afraid to venture out into night, infested   -
with ghosts and devils, ghosts that strangle
one, ghosts from far-away villages, ghosts who
leap upon the back and may not be shaken
off.

107   "olden days . . . he might take a club and   -
together with his relatives go out and kill
those who sit without."

"the peaceful teachings of Christianity . . .   +
have made far less change in the belligerent
activities of the women than in those of the
men."

109   conflict between the rank of a woman's   -
brother and that of her husband.

125   "oppressive atmosphere of the small town is   -
all about them."

"This glaring publicity is compensated for by   -
a violent gloomy secretiveness."

139   (ten-year-old) Pele: despite burdens, "attitude   +
towards life was essentially gay and sane."

140   "pair of hotheaded children."   -

"less given to gratuitous outlays of personal   -
service."

"Tuna's task much harder."   -

"But she reaped her reward in the slightly   +
extra gentleness with which they treated their
most burdened associate."

141   Ula (pre-ad): "alert, pretty pampered."   +

142   Lalala: "cruel public defloration ceremony."   -

"Fitu combined a passionate devotion to her   +
mother . . . "

"Fitu [midway] was often teased by her   -
mother and rebuked by her companions for
being like a boy."

143   "Fitu [midway] bossed and joked with her   -
mother in a fashion shocking to all Samoan
onlookers."

147 Talo (ad): "obvious sophistication and win- +
ning charm."

"friendship between these two girls." +

154 devoted maiden aunt, docile, never resented +
work, babies, etc.

156 Sila (adult): "her fury knew no bounds." -

158–59 "Violent outbursts of wrath and summary -
chastisements do occur but consistant and
prolonged disciplinary measures are absent."

159 Within the same age-category tolerance is not -
so tempered.

Children accept physical defects and "slight +
strangeness of temperament."

160 Cases of passionate jealousy occur . . . only - -
cases in nine months: girl informed against
faithless lover, girl bit off part rival's ear,
woman whose husband deserted her fought
and severly injured her successor, girl falsely
accused a rival of stealing (see 156 and 177
for the last two incidents).

165 Sona (ad): "overbearing in manner, arbitrary - -
and tyrannous towards young people, impu-
dently deferential towards her elders."

166 Manita (adult): haughty and aggressive nature. -

168 Father of Ana (ad) of Siufaga: gentle retiring +
man.

Mother greatly mistrusts men. -

Aunts continually harping—Ana too weak. -

170 "slightly Europeanized state is replete with +
easy solutions for all conflicts."

173   Lola (ad, delinquent): strong feelings, violent   -
      responses.

      Mother kindly.   +

      Sami mild and gentle like mother but soft   +
      undercurrent of resentment.

      Lola's mother ineffective.   -

174   Lola (ad, delinquent): quarrelsome, insubor-   -
      dinate, impertinent . . . stormy scenes at
      pastors; etc.

175   Lola (ad, delinquent): "became bored, sullen,   -
      jealous."

177   Lola (ad, delinquent): rage unbounded, re-   -
      venge, accuses rival of theft; driven out.

178   Lola (ad, delinquent): branded *lotu le aga*   -
      (jealous, envious).

      Mala (ad, delinquent): treacherous, stole, lied   - -
      played with boys (see page 179).

      Lola: "living idle, sullen and defiant."   -

      Mala: "None showed Mala any affection, and   - -
      they worked her unmercifully."

179   Mala (ad, delinquent): "early childhood she   -
      had been branded as a thief."

      "Her first offense had been to steal a foreign   -
      toy."

      Played with boys, etc. "This behavior was   -
      displayed to the whole village who were
      vociferous in their condemnation."

      "They teased her, bullied her, used her as   -
      general errand boy and fag."

180 "Lola and Mala both seemed to be the victims of lack of affection."   -

Lola had a double handicap in her unfortunate temperament.   -

"seldom were children as desolate as Mala."   -

181 Sala (ad, delinquent): with pastor but involved in sex and expelled.   -

Attitude toward pastor unveiled hostility.   -

Stupid, underhanded, deceitful father beat her occasionally half-hearted manner.   -

182 (Eleven-year-old) Lola and sister Siva (similar): fist fights, deadly insults; mimicry, humor.   -

183 Siva (pre-ad): mad not chosen for first dance, doubles up fists.   -

190 "The young married women twenty to thirty are a busy, cheerful group."   +

192 Father angry that his title was given to me and would tell me nothing.   -

198 "General casualness of the whole society."   +

"no one plays for very high stakes, no one pays very heavy prices, no one suffers for his convictions or fights to the death for special ends."   +

Disagreements: parents-child moving, men move next village, *ifoga* seducer.   +++

Neither poverty nor great disasters.   ++

No implacable gods with swift anger, strong punishment.   +

Wars, cannibalism long gone.   +

199   "No one is hurried along in life or punished   +
harshly for slowness of development."

"Lola and Mala and little Siva, Lola's sister, - -
all were girls with a capacity for emotion
greater than their fellows. And Lola and Mala,
passionately desiring affection and too vio-
lently venting upon the community their
disappointment over their lack of it, were
both delinquent, unhappy misfits in a society
which gave all the rewards to those who took
defeat lightly and turned to some other goal
with a smile."

277   "mercy of God without the doctrine of   +
original sin."

News Bulletins

September 14, 1925

(Mrs. Sua, Samoan principal of the Poyer - +
school): "She smiles sweetly and tells her
children she is certainly going to whip them
but she never does."

October 1, 1925

Court: "one school girl had bitten off an- -
other's ear."

"the mother of her who had been bitten rose -
and demanded veangance declaring that Suli
was her only child and that she would rather
die than have her lose her ear and also than
have the perpetrator of the crime go so lightly
punished."

October 7, 1925

> Still Tutuila: "Also the fact that all the   -
> sanctions are social rather than religious
> seems to rob the culture of depth and
> intensity. The old tapus, never strong, have
> practically no force now, and a diluted
> Christianity, which consists mainly in the
> singing of impossible hymns and the praying
> of lengthy dull prayers, adds no glamour to
> the life. The whole thing is a life curiously
> lacking in depth, no dark malignant spirits
> prowl behind simple activities, graves are
> neglected in a year, rank is hedged about not
> with tapus, but with hairpulling, and the
> deepest crime is to make a mistake in a mans
> courtesy title. It is much easier to derive
> aesthetic pleasure from contemplating the
> ideas underlying their culture than from
> looking at the human embodiments of these
> ideas."

October 31, 1925

> "I asked Faamotu [a *tāupou* and a daughter   -
> of Ufuti] if Pupa [sister of Ufuti] was married
> and the softest saddest voice in the world,
> whispered, "ua uma" [it's finished], and
> added that her husband had gone to Upolo
> and never returned and that her three
> children were dead."

> "And the kind consideration with which the   +
> children almost insisted on Pupa's dancing,
> etc. was sweet to see."

November 14, 1925

> maid of Holts, "Sila": "Her husband has   - - -
> deserted her, her baby is dead; . . . and makes
> faces behind the FoMa'i's (doctor's) back."

December 11, 1925

> Pele (pre-ad): "with soft brown curls and the   +
> gentlest expression in the world."

> Maliu, (midway): "does not have a loto leaga   +
> (jealous heart)."

> Fitu (midway): "the only really cross, cranky   -
> little creature who likes to hit the other
> children over the head with my fan if they
> open their mouths. I have to tell her a dozen
> times a day "le pule 'oe," which is really "you
> aren't the boss."

> Timu (pre-ad): "who has white blood, is the   -
> prettiest child in the three villages but pays
> for her beautifully shaped little face and small
> hands and feet with a terrific shyness."

December 20, 1925

> "Max Halleck, the German . . . came over on   -
> the leone . . . And in addition there was a
> heavy strain in the air. Max has a Samoan
> wife; [a *matai*] is the father of one of Max's
> children. They sat and glared at each other,
> [the *matai*] with a gay insolence which he
> wears well despite his two hundred and fifty
> pounds; Max irritable and blond, telling [the
> *matai*] that no-one in Germany, from whence
> he has just returned, had ever heard of
> Samoa."

"or inquiring into the . . . methods by which —
jealous wives amputate their rivals ears."

January 2, 1926

"the great basket of presents were brought —
out and distributed, the spoils, and Christmas
was over—all but the aftermath which consisted mainly of complaints that presents had
been lost . . . Came one, came many
complaining that theirs had been lost. It was
death to listen for we were already stripped
to the very bone, and furthermore this an old
trick to get two gifts. But it made one very
uncomfortable. They also have two other
charming little ways, to tell you how beautiful
your gift to someone else is and to dwell
lingerly on the beauty of the gift which they
gave to you, carefully abstaining the while
from referring to their own gift. The [village
official] . . . came over the next morning and
converses lengthily with me while I was
putting away my treasures. "Lelei Samoa, tele
mea alofo tele. Leaga papalagi, laititi ana mea
alofa." (Samoa is good, the Samoans give
many large gifts, but the papalagi's are cheap
skates giving little)."

"laid [the official] low for some fifteen +
minutes . . . the official stayed all morning,
very docile and repentant."

January 23

"[Malae] was X's interpreter but the defen- —
dant mistrusted him . . . So they compromised
on me."

"He was determined that "Malae" shouldn't   -
speak at all, and still "Malae" is the highest
chief in Tau and he had to be polite to him
. . . he would blurt out dancing about in his
impotent rage."

"Malae" has "passed", as they say. He got   -
drunk and sassed the Judge and now he is
suspended for six months."

"argued with members of the Aumaga (the   -
young men) on the advisability of burning
down what is left of Ofu, becuase the people
of Ofu stoned the meddlesome pastor of Tau
out of the village."

February 9, 1926

"At midnight [Sona, adolescent] comes in   -
from the reef with a cut on her back which
a very very bad boy has given her with a great
great great big stone and I must needst
bandage it."

February 14, 1926

"[a *matai*] has come to send a wireless   - +
message that his daughter was dead . . . he
stayed the two hours and we engaged in slow
sorrowful converse until he got interested in
discussing the glorious days when there was
a TuiManu'a and he lost both grief-stricken
mien and chiefly dignity in the enthusiasm
with which he demonstrated, with the help
of a tin cup, the top of a powder box and
wash basin, the eleven fold Kava ceremony of
the TuiManu'a."

"We had a lovely instance of professional   -
pride the other night. There was a new baby
and one of the nurses got Mr. Holt [the naval
medical officer] to come over and look at it.
When he entered the house the old Samoan
midwife, who is by the way the high chief's
sister, turned her back on him and sat in
haughty offended withdrawal until he left."

March 7, 1926

And I've listened to my talking chiefs quarrel   -
and scheme over the return presents and
shared the humiliation of high chiefs too poor
to properly validate their privileges."

"Only this feminine kava ceremony was a   +
gayer matter."

March 24, 1926

Life in Ofu was complicated by the fact that   -
there is a famine."

"Olosega was wrecked by the hurricane. There   -
will be no copra for years, And there is
nothing to eat except Masi."

"So the village was churlish, took our short   -
stay in ill part."

"Our gracious hosts killed a pig for us and   +
the whole tiny village made merry, while the
high chiefs told me anecdotes, illustrated, of
the day of cannibalism . . . "

Fieldnotes

November 11, 1925

female adolescent: Character sketches household members (in translation):

(adult untitled man) "He does not anger
easily."   +

(adult woman) "She does not get angry." "She   ++
does not scold."

(adult woman) "Her behavior is good."   +

(adult woman) "Her behavior is good."   +

(adolescent boy) "Has consideration for   +
everyone."

(adult woman) "Her conduct is good." "She   +++
is considerate." Of herself: "She loves her
sisters and everyone."

(adult male) "His behavior is good and he is   +
considerate."

(adult woman) "Her conduct is good and she   ++
is considerate." "She doesn't get angry easily."

(adult male) "He is considerate." "He is   +++
mild-mannered (agamalu)." "He does not
scold." "He doesn't get angry easily."

(adult woman) "Her husband is dead." "She   - +
does not smile often." "She is considerate."

(female adolescent) "She is very considerate."   ++
"She is kind to people who come to visit the
family."

January 20, 1926

> "[Mutu] was to perform the autopsy and — -
> remove the foetus and there was considerable
> controversy over this as he had been at enmity
> with the family for a month over his intrigue
> with [Moana]."

Typed March 22, 1928

> [a *matai*]:

> "[another *matai*] has no guest house because —
> of a quarrel in the family. (Later there was a
> great deal of commotion over this, the young
> unsuccessful rival to the title tried to build a
> house on the malae sacred to the house of
> [the *matai*]."

> "The young men of Siufaga laid waste the —
> taro plantation of Luma, then their own faded
> and died and they had to have a kava
> confessional of sin to cast off curse."

Typed March 29, 1928

> "[a young man] knew of two bluebeards, one —
> killed three wives."

Binder

1   (11, pre-ad) "A shy overworked [?]quiescent — -
    joyless child, encumbered with babies."

2   (9, pre-ad) "A mother with a perfectly vile —
    temper—always beating [her] . . . battered
    from pillar to post."

    "[?]cheerfully."   +

3   (9, pre-ad) "a horrible baby, completely   -
impossible, [?]stinking. Retarded mentally
and emotionally."

4   (12, pre-ad) "devoted to her mother."   +

mother "[?]changed form joyous defiant crea- -
ture into a [?]horrible looking rag since the
death of her baby."

[twelve-year-old] "strangely sullen [?]about it." -

"sloppy moody, [?]sort of a child."   -

"some delinquents": [Pele] "[?]devious little -
[?]monster."

[Siva] mw: "unruly young devil."   -

"virtuous enslaved."   -

[Mala] (ad): "rebellious against [?]conditions." -

5   pre-ads: "a general hostility & jealousy."   -

"[?]constant [?]scene [?]of fighting, teasing etc." -

adolescents (younger): "self-conscious, awk- -
ward, incessant giggling, very sudden [?]as-
sension of selfconsiousness-loss of the
[?]perfect control."

7   "very old treated deferentially—but in accord- +
ance with rank."

8   [Sila] "says married when 15 against her will." -

"husband used to beat her every night."   -

"so she left him and came back to her real parents with her little boy whom she loved." +

"she did live in pastor's house but was [?]banished." -

"she's a stupid girl—[?]cannot weave anything." -

9   [Ula], 10. "beloved younger sister of ? . . ." +

"her [?]mothers favorite." +

"Loves [sister] but she is too cross." + -

[Maliu & Fitu] mw. "dear friends"; "na'o le aiga = [only family]." +

[?] [?] dear friends. +

[?]teases Fitu. -

if a girl sleeps with two boys in one night, the first one is angry and fights with second." [told by two males, 16 & 33]. -

10   m of Talo, fem adult: "vain, young, [?]conceited, devoted to children, strict." +

f young [?] [?]mild manners. +

"Talo": "oedipus comp." [Selu] mw: "vale" [stupid], "continually rebukes ["Ana"] ad also for [?]noisiness." -

"Fitu," mw, "excessive devotion to mother." -

"good natured." +

"heavily charged [?]bickering back & forth."   -

[?] do of [?] in S "is unwilling to marry a ff   -
who has T.B. She ran away to . . . Soon her
parents will [?]have her again."

11   . . . "dislike [Lola] ad."   -

12   [Selu] mw, "She is good."   +

20   [Pala] ad, "This and her bashfulness seem to   -
incite the Taulealeas to [?]teasing, in the face
of which she is helpless."

"dislikes x's baby."   -

"has no great affection for her worthless   -
mother." [prostitute].

21   [Aso] ad, "devoted to her older sister and to   +
her sister's baby."

"like [Sami] [fem of twenty-four] takes a   +
rather non-combative attitude toward life."

"both [Lola] ad. and [?] are too much for   -
her."

34   "Father is beneficent but dumb apparently   +
very dumb."

"Mother is tolerant, [?]kindly."   +

"In moment of stress turns the baby over to   -
[Lua] ad, who is extremely overworked."

"mother is proud of training nine living children." +

35 x, m of [Vina] ad & [Ana] "fond of her children." +

"Christlike face gentle, kindly ceremonious. . . . Most cordial welcome in Tau." +

"x [mw not in text] is willing, cheerful, untalkative." +

"Honest, friendly." +

36 "[Mala] ad, "left [ff school] because ["Lola"] ad [del] beat her. -

regarding x, male of 16: "she has watched his ways was afraid to go home when x did." -

"Is stupid, goodnatured." +

38 [Lola] ad, del, "hoyden." "displeased [Pusa] wife of [Fua]." -

who was too strict and worked everyone to death so ran away." -

"She is not liked by her two sisters." -

"when she lived at [Fua's] didn't get on with them. Quarreled continually." -

"now at x's doesn't get on with [Pula] mw." -

[Pula] mw, "is an obstreperous midway." -

"She is of a quarrelsome, [?] noisy disposition." -

"She's jealous, [?] violent."   -

39   x, ad, "Faithful, reliable, good judgment.   ++
      Neither boasts nor lies."

      "takes great joy in their [?]successes."   +

40   [Lola] ad, del: "kicked out by x, m of y."   -

      "[?] furiously disliked by [Sami], twenty-four-   -
      year-old."

      "Openly defies her [mother] & [Sami]."   -

      "pouts, refuses to do things."   -

      "Disliked by village. . . . " "gets violent." [Siva]   -
      "had the same temperment exactly." mw

44   [Mina] fem 20, "cherishes neither violent   +
      enthusiasm nor dislikes."

45   [Moana] ad, 15, matai says "that she had been   -
      misbehaving."

      "accepts [Sila's] loving sisterly attentions as   +
      tributes to her superior good looks."

47   [Mina] fem, 20, "not given to quarreling or   +
      gossiping."

48   [Luina], fem ad, 17, "Disliked by other girls   -
      because she's stupid & imperious and dis-
      agreeable."

      "shy, suspicious, greedy."   -

Bibliography

Augustine, Saint. 1872 (5th century A.D.). *The City of God.* 2 vols. Edinburgh: T. & T. Clark.

Benedict, Ruth. 1928. Review of: *Coming of Age in Samoa,* by Margaret Mead (New York: Morrow, 1928). *Journal of Philosophy* 26:110.

Blalock, Hubert M., Jr. 1972. *Social Statistics.* New York: McGraw Hill.

Boas, Franz. 1928. "Foreword," in *Coming of Age in Samoa.* New York: Morrow.

Brady, Ivan, ed. 1983. "Speaking in the Name of the Real: Freeman and Mead on Samoa." *American Anthropologist* 85:908–47.

Calvin, John. 1960 (1545). *Institutes of the Christian Religion.* Philadelphia: Westmister Press.

Copp, John, and Fa'afouina I. Pula. 1950. *Samoan Dance of Life.* Boston: Beacon Press.

Dillon, Wilton. 1980. "Mead and Government." *American Anthropologist* 82:319–39

Ellis, Havelock. 1929. "Introduction," in *Sex in Civilization*. Ed. V. F. Calverton and S. D. Schmalhausen. London: Macauley.

Feinberg, Richard. 1988. "Margaret Mead and Samoa: Coming of Age in Fact and Fiction." *American Anthropologist* 90:656–63.

Freeman, Derek. 1966. "Anthropological Theorizing and Historical Scholarship: A Reply to M. Ember." *American Anthropologist* 68:168–71.

———. 1972. "Social Organization of Manu'a by Margaret Mead: Some Errata." *Journal of Polynesian Society* 81:70–78.

———. 1983a. *Margaret Mead and Samoa: The Making and Unmaking of an Anthropological Myth*. Cambridge: Harvard University Press.

———. 1983b. "Inductivism and the Test of Truth: A Rejoinder to Lowell D. Holmes and Others," pp. 101–92, in *Fact and Context in Ethnography: The Samoa Controversy*. Canberra Anthropology 6 (2).

———. 1989. "Fa'apua'a Fa'amu and Margaret Mead." *American Anthropologist* 91:1017–22.

———. Spring, 1991. "There's Tricks i' th' World: An Historical Analyisis of the Samoan Researches of Margaret Mead." *Visual Anthropology Review*. American Anthropological Association. Volume 7, Number 1.

Gardiner, Martin. 1993. The Great Samoan Hoax. *Skeptical Inquirer*, Winter, 131–35.

Gerber, Eleanor. 1975. The Cultural Patterning of Emotions in Samoa. PhD. diss. University of California, San Diego.

Gordon, Joan, ed. 1976. *Margaret Mead: The Complete Bibliography 1925–1975*. The Hague-Paris: Mouton.

Hall, G. Stanley. 1904. *Adolescence, its Psychology and Its Relations to Physiology, Anthropology, Sociology: Sex, Crime, Religion, and*

Education. New York: D. Appleton.

Heimans, Frank. 1988. *Margaret Mead and Samoa*. Film. Sydney: Cinetel Productions.

Holmes, Lowell D. 1957. *A Restudy of Manu'an Culture: A Problem in Methodology*. Ph.D. diss. Northwestern University.

———. 1958. *Ta'u: Stability and Change in a Samoan Village*. Wellington, New Zealand: Polynesian Society.

———. 1987. *Quest for the Real Samoa*. South Hadley: Bergin and Garvey.

Honigmann, John J. 1963. *Understanding Culture*. New York: Harper and Row.

Konner, Melvin. 1982. *The Tangled Wing*. New York: Holt, Rinehart, and Winston.

———. 1990. *Why the Reckless Survive, and Other Secrets of Human Nature*. New York: Penguin Books.

Lederer, William J., and Eugene W. Burdick. 1958. *The Ugly American*. New York: Norton.

Lowie, Robert. 1929. Review of: *Coming of Age in Samoa*, by Margaret Mead (New York: Morrow, 1928). *American Anthropologist* 31:532–34.

Mead, Margaret. 1973 (1928). *Coming of Age in Samoa*. New York: Morrow.

———. 1928. "The Role of the Individual in Samoan Culture." *Journal of the Royal Anthropological Institute* 58:481–95.

———. 1929. "Americanization in Samoa." *American Mercury* 16:264–70.

———. 1969 (1930). *Social Organization of Manu'a*. Bernice P. Bishop Museum Bulletin 76.

———. 1937. *Cooperation and Competition Among Primitive Peoples*.

New York: McGraw-Hill.

———. 1939. *From the South Seas: Studies of Adolescence and Sex in Primitive Societies.* New York: Morrow.

———. 1960 (1955). *Male and Female: A Study of the Sexes in a Changing World.* New York: Mentor Books, New American Library of World Literature.

Milner, G. B. 1966. *Samoan Dictionary.* London: Oxford University Press.

Popper, Karl. 1968 (1966) 2d edition. *The Logic of Scientific Discovery.* New York: Harper and Row.

Pratt, George. 1977 (1862). *Pratt's Grammar and Dictionary of the Samoan Language.* Apia, Western Samoa: Malua Printing Press.

Russell, Bertrand. 1957 (1929). *Marriage and Morals.* New York: Liveright.

Schoeffel, P., and M. Meleisea. 1983. "Derek Freeman and Samoa," pp. 58–69, in *Fact and Context in Ethnography: The Samoan Controversy.* Canberra Anthropology 6 (2).

Schwartz, Theodore. 1983. "Anthropology: A Quaint Science." *American Anthropologist* 85:919–28.

Shore, Bradd. 1982. *Sala'ilua, a Samoan Mystery.* New York: Columbia University Press.

———. 1983. "Paradox Regained. Freeman's Margaret Mead and Samoa." *American Anthropologist* 85:935–44.

Tawney, Richard Henry. 1961 (1926). *Religion and the Rise of Capitalism.* New York: Mentor Books, New American Library of World Literature.

Weiner, Annette B. 1983. "Ethnographic Determinism: Samoa and the Margaret Mead Controversy." *American Anthropologist* 85:909–19.

Index

Abortion, 52, 61, 66

Adolescence, 1–4, 12; biological determination and, 29; characteristics of in the U.S. in the 1920's, 28; idealism and philosophical perplexities in, 29; positive versus negative statements about in Samoan data, 115; stress in, 5, 9, 12, 29, 96, 102, 120, 123, 135, 140, 153–157. *See also* Affect (diffusion of), Girls, Sexual experience

Adolescents. *See* Girls

Adultery, 61, 64, 65, 88, 104, 139

Affect, diffusion of, 30, 106, 108, 116, 153

Age, as limitation on free love, 78, 141

Agonistic Samoa, 5, 10, 12, 16, 106, 110–121, 150–155. *See also* Beatings, Competition, Halcyon Samoa, Political (turmoil), Rape, Sanctions, Stoning, Violence

'Aigā, aiga, 49, 61, 66

Ali'i. *See* Chiefs

American Anthropologist, 3, 9

"Amigo," 50, 99

Anger, 119

Anthropologists, 6, 7, 11, 18, 124, 126, 137, 157

Anthropology, 5, 28, 131–135, 156; cultural, 6, 7, 10–13, 125, 131, 152. *See also* Science

Apia (capital of Western Samoa), 105, 112

Argument, Mead's, 28–32, 108, 120, 123, 128, 131, 135, 139, 147, 148, 154, 155; theoretical presuppositions of Mead, 29; contradictory, 133. *See also* Evidence, Generalization, "Not even wrong," Reliability, Verifiability

Atauloma, girls school, 19; teacher interview, 54–56, 85, 86, 146

Aunu'u (American Samoan island), 17

183